Reviews for *Clean Love*

"Using a sword of truth, *Clean Love* cuts away all that is not pure in the realm of love. *Clean Love* gets to the deepest places within our hearts and exposes our vulnerable truth, separating us from our sometimes deceitful ego. *Clean Love* is full of vital truths and practical suggestions for healing relationships, which inspire us to live from the inside out as soul-connected, risk taking believers in God's unconditional Love."

—Dan Russell, *singer songwriter and Producer of SoulFest*

"This book inspires us to take a less cynical look at ourselves and humanity as together, we seek to find the systemic problems affecting all of us today.

The writer suggests thriving in life rather than just surviving life. As the reader progresses through the chapters, they are given practical steps and examples in various scenarios to learn how to let go of unnecessary pain and find healing.

This book rightly suggests that asking God for a clean heart is His way of offering an internal remodel providing the necessary renewal needed for positive change.

Gina Blaze also shows us how to keep remembering to circle back in order to sustain our newly found thriving lifestyle.

Remember when you are stuck in life, a supporting hand is always welcome and with faith and this book in hand you don't have to go it alone."

—Thomas C. Walker, *National Governors Prayer Team*

I had the great privilege of seeing the process of *Clean Love* come forth. This book is the creative extension of a heart who has experienced love in its purest of forms. *Clean Love* drives you to the awareness of what you are allowing in your life, it is a call to something greater and a tool for the days at hand. *Clean Love* will leave you wanting more of the Love that knows no limits or bounds and in turn will push you to pour it out on this world that desperately needs the truth of love.

—Lindsay Blaze, *Daughter, Creative, Lover of Life*

A Note About the Cover

The artist, Greg Rudd combines his creativity and talent of art with prayer. With every brush stroke and thought of color, Greg captured the title in art of "Clean Love" for the cover of this book. For over 30 years Greg and I have shared many heartfelt prayers with each other and now we get to share the words and artistry of *Clean Love*. What a gift!

Greg describes the painting this way:

"There is a hidden meaning of symbolism on the cover of this book. The sunrise is the birth of a new dawn, God's love and faithfulness giving us new mercies every morning. The light from the horizon represents God's passion for all people and the clouds represent His redemptive love for us. The waterfall has three distinct sections symbolizing the Father, Son, and the Holy Spirit. The Source of Clean Love."

CLEAN
LOVE

WHAT THE WORLD NEEDS NOW

GINA BLAZE

During the publication process of this book, my brother, Ralph, passed away suddenly. Part of his story is in the book. His lifelong suffering played a big part in the path of my life. A lot of what I learned about love was birthed from his longsuffering. In a world where people judge the outward appearance, and cruelty has no conviction, Ralph paved a trail for many to practice empathy, kindness, love, and mercy. Beyond his illness and behind the torment and ravaging of his life, lived a person that deserved dignity and honor. Anyone who reads this book, gives it any praise, or gains any perspective from it, that honor goes to you, Ralph.

Dedication

A dedication is really meant to be a blessing, not in disguise, but in full view for all the world to see. We all have a temporary stay here and it's what we do with what we have that's important. This book is what I have and I dedicate it to you . . . lovers and haters, colors and cultures, creeds and genders, to all people in every nation.

There is a time and season of glory for every purpose under heaven. When something stands the test of time, it validates authenticity. Truth has stood for thousands of years. The truth will always bring safety, success, and increase to life. In this moment in history we need the truth more than anything. I wrote the truth in this book for you.

So, my new friends, I dedicate and celebrate you with this book. Your life matters and it's my prayer to refresh the memory in your spirit with the truth of the strongest force in all the world:

LOVE.

I dedicate this book to you.

Table of Contents

Foreword

Who doesn't enjoy reading heartwarming love stories, receiving a love-laced card, opening an "I-love-you" email, or watching a happy-ever-after, love-themed movie? If you live long enough, you will meet lovely people and friends who will help you write the most beautiful stories filled with love on the pages of time and in your diary called life. Life, however, when compared to scripted love stories in movies or novels, doesn't always have a happy every after. The real-life counterpart is riddled with broken hearts and bruised emotions. However, in the following pages of *Clean Love*, you will discover heartwarming short love stories and anecdotes from real-life events that will not only inspire you, but also put warmth in your heart and hopefully a fire in your soul.

A 21st-century book on an age-old virtue, Gina Blaze's treatment of this topic is soul stirring and affirming. She engages us from start to finish; keeping us, the reader, captivated with her stories and anecdotes. *Clean Love* finds relevance in a world where the word "love" is recklessly used to describe just about any type of human affinity: from the love of sushi to the love of a brand of sneakers. Blaze does an amazing job in elevating the word love back to its origin—the heart of God himself.

In this refreshing look at love, Gina does a great job at highlighting the greatest power on earth, while also revealing love's manifold expressions. Some of these stories will make you laugh, others will make you cry, yet all will deeply convince you of the ever-abiding, limitless power of God's love—and how it is the empowering force enabling us to overcome every obstacle. Truly, what the world needs now is love sweet love!

I read a beautiful story that depicts the eternal, sweet love of God, which I shall recount with my own imaginary and cinematic-quality mental twist. The plot and characters have been changed to increase impact and to reinforce the message herein contained. One day, a young bride received a beautiful bouquet of flowers from her husband who had been deployed to Iraq. In it, she counted thirteen flowers accompanied by a short note. It was written in beautiful lettering and read: "My love for you will last until the day the last flower in this bouquet dies. Until we are together again, may this flower comfort you in the moments when missing me gives you emotional pain. In those moments, look at that flower and remember that I love you eternally." Unsure as to what to make of the message, especially knowing how dangerous his mission was, she went home in the evening and placed the flowers in water. After a week, one by one, the flowers began to whither, until only one remained. That was the day when she took a good look and realized that there was one artificial flower in the bouquet that would last forever. Her husband did return and they lived happily ever after. On their twentieth anniversary, she asked him, "Why did you give me thirteen roses and not a dozen?" He answered, "Because the greatest text about love is found in 1st Corinthians 13: the thirteenth verse states, "Now abides faith, hope, and love, but the greatest of these is love." My love for you, my darling, abides forever!"

Love is eternal, because the eternal God is love. *Clean Love* reminds us of the awe-inspiring beauty, power, and strength of God's love for us and in us. A delightful and edifying read, I see this book as a gentle challenge for every believer to rethink how they love.

—Dr. Cindy Trimm, CEO/Life-strategist,
Bestselling Author, Humanitarian

Acknowledgments

If you met Kim Torre-Tasso, I promise, you would immediately know that Kim is beautiful, healthy, pure, and smart. She loves her family and friends with a deep commitment to arise and shine in spite of life's tough circumstances. She is responsible, professional, caring, and kind. Kim wants others to be blessed. She has supported me like a midwife as I have labored to push out this book. She has been a great source of encouragement and has dropped everything to help me. She edited and corrected *Clean Love*. Thank you, Kim, I am eternally grateful.

Cindy Trimm—I have known you most through the reading of your books. *Declaring Your Morning* changed me. When I called you about this book, I knew I would be given absolute honesty and wisdom. Thank you for stretching me to the "exceedingly abundantly more" place, so that I could birth a healthier writing. God made "Great Lights" to shine beautiful and brilliant to light the day and light the darkness. You shine beautiful and brilliant. Thank you for speaking life into me and into this book.

Dan, my man. . . . Through thick and thin, storm or sun, you never change. You're always happy. Throughout the writing of this book, you have shown me unconditional grace. Hours and hours of time, days and weeks we could have been together—you sacrificed for *Clean Love*. You listened tirelessly to new changes and thoughts. You are always a step ahead, with a cup of encouragement and a fresh coffee, an a neck massage. You always know what is needed. You have lived fully persuaded that nothing, absolutely nothing, will separate us from each other or God. Clean love is your life. I am so blessed. Thank you, I love you.

Lindsay Blaze, my weeks in Tennessee not only gave me the opportunity to write with no distractions, but the gift of time with you. You keep surprising me. God uses you to help people see what clean love looks like, without judgment. Thank you for helping me *see*. Blessed are the pure in heart; surely your heart is pure. I love you.

D.B. and Dayna—I apologize that I have not been present during the writing of this book—thank you for understanding. I may have been preoccupied with writing, but get ready, now that it's finished—here I come! Watching the two of you raise Luka and Lainey has been the delight of my heart. Your clean love for each other and those children complements life and family. You are affecting so many. Thank you, I love you.

Preface

Love is the greatest thing in the world. It's the most powerful force in all the world. It contains joy, hope, peace, promise and freedom. Love can transform any life. The one short phrase that describes love with the greatest accuracy: "God is Love."

The Secret of Love

Love is way bigger than we understand. It's wider and longer and deeper and higher. I am still trying to find the words to show its immensity. It may be best understood by the vastness of the ocean or the great expanse of the galaxies. Man has not scratched the surface in the discoveries of these secret worlds. Volumes and volumes of research and libraries with shelves of knowledge on these subjects are just the tip of what we know about the depths of the sea and the heights of the cosmos. Both ocean and space life are distinct from land life. There is an elaborate, raw, magnificent, wilderness of complexity yet to be explored. That is how love is. It's deeper than the depths and higher than the heights and every day there are new discoveries to be made about love.

The life of love is completely separate from customary life. Love thrives on forgiveness, healing, redemption, encouragement, and compassion. We have been thoroughly created for love and yet we have not come into its full identity. We cannot measure love through the lens of ministry, theology, talents, exploits, or money. Love is in the soul of every man, in the deepest place. All of our self-efforts and self-solutions keep us striving hard to try and prosper our souls with love. Love's soul secret to prospering is resting in God. When the soul is filled with contentment in God, the need for self-striving ends and the increase of life begins.

There is a discovery I made in my quest to search out the enormity of love. The tiniest grain of sand is almost microscopic. Yet tiny grains together form outstretched magnificent beaches across the world. Grains of sand can never be counted, because every day, all day long, sand is being formed by waves, wind, and rain hitting rocks. More and more and more of these tiny grains keep forming. From sunrise to sunset they keep forming. They are unstoppable. That is the way love is. God's thoughts of love toward us are so much more than the grains of sand. They keep forming every day, all day. Right this very second, they are forming. When our souls overflow with those elaborate, raw, magnificent grains of love, we rest in the unstoppable, untamable, never ending Love of God.

Introduction

Life's journey reveals what we like and what we don't. Along my journey, I discovered that I like to write. During the 2020 COVID-19 quarantine, I decided to use my time to finish this book, which I had started years ago. If timing is everything, I am sure this book's time has come. For me, it's like the piece of a puzzle that finishes the board. As I sit at my writing desk, the world is in the middle of a pandemic, protests and race riots have become the new normal, and fear and confusion abound. The issues we face today are myriad, and the roots of these struggles run deep. These issues highlight that we are a generation that could benefit from examining our hearts.

What we are seeing around the world is an outward reaction to an inward problem. Most people are unaware it exists. It's gone undiagnosed far too long and this internal SOS call happening in people today is the real pandemic. Life has taken many of us down the road of constantly trying to fix our outward appearance when all along there is a systemic internal problem affecting all of humanity. Individual renovation and renewal are needed on the *inside*. The urgent unspoken call for help in the hearts of people called this book into being.

Clean love is God's essential business to refocus us on what's most important. It's the answer to stop the plague of hate in us. The purpose of this purification process is *to create in us a clean heart*. The power from His waterfall of love will break down the boulders that divide us. The world needs it now, people need it now, you need it now. You're worth it.

The Pandemic of Love

Nobody ever dreamed in the year 2020 we would be living in the middle of a pandemic and a time where wearing masks in public would be required. COVID-19 has left a lot of people hopeless, insecure, confused, terrified, angry, and worried about the future. It has taken people's jobs, money, and freedoms away. It has divided and separated people, taken hundreds of thousands of precious lives, and broken the hearts of millions of families. There is every kind of medical opinion, discussion, and theory out there on COVID-19 and they are all so very different. The news changes every day and confusion reigns. People are searching for the real truth.

A long time ago, a governor named Pontius Pilate asked a very important question. He asked, "What is truth?" All over the earth people are driven by their truth. They are passionate about living by the rules of their truth; others are breaking every rule because of it.

So, what is truth?

Love is truth.

In spite of everything COVID has taken away, what it doesn't take away is your love. If anything good has come out of the pandemic so far, it has shown all of us what's really important in life and what's not. It has caused people to treat time and others differently, to pray more, to do intentional acts of kindness, to evaluate life, and to prepare more for the future. People have gone beyond what is usual and ordinary to show others their love. We have all watched with admiration and smiles the coverage of "good news" that shows people going to extreme lengths to display their love. Outside of nursing homes, at hospitals, in neighborhoods, restaurants, and on the streets—people have gone to extraordinary measures to exhibit their love to a family member, friend, or stranger, all for one reason—because *love never fails.*

COVID-19 has tried to do its worst, but for many it has brought the best out by growing love inside of them. Those who know God's truth wake up every morning with a smile on their face; they know "Love is the key, love is the answer. Love is the greatest tool and love is the greatest weapon."

COVID-19 will eventually go away, but love will never die. There are over eight thousand promises of love that God gave to humanity in scripture and in one of those promises it says, "My words will never pass away."

Who Am I?

Who am I, and why should my perspective and advice be useful to you? As a Life Coach, I am in the people field . . . *gleaning*. Years ago, I wrote a course called "Alive on the Inside." Over the years of coaching many people, I can honestly tell you that God has honed me. "Alive on the Inside" brings out the brilliance, excellence, and value inside of people that's been hidden from themselves.

In addition to coaching, I am the director of a hope and healing center with its foundation in prayer (The New England Prayer Center), located in Connecticut. I am also a guest speaker to churches, corporations, and home groups of all sizes (nationally and internationally). I hold a deep responsibility to extend to others what's been extended to me.

I've come to learn that everybody has a story inside of them, waiting and wanting to be heard, birthed out of pain or passion, often without a title. Our titles don't define us, but the stories we carry do. I have been privileged to help people better understand how to love themselves. A new perspective helps people transition from the "pit to the palace," ridding despair and moving toward real peace and wholeness on the inside.

There is no denying that my heart belongs to Jesus, and as I write this book it comes from a place of passion for *all* people. It is my fervent prayer that this book fulfills its purpose. I pray that people will ponder the words on these pages as much as I pondered the writing. As you read, this book will read you. Reading is a choice and knowledge is power and it is my heart's cry that if you choose to spend time on these pages, you will find value in the words found here. I am grateful and humbled if you do, but if not, I am still happy that the book caught your attention. Please know that if your hands touch this book, your heart has been prayed for.

Disclaimer: This book is written for those who are ready to let go of unnecessary pain and experience the blessing of Clean Love.

CHAPTER 1

THE HEART OF THE MATTER

Built for Love

WE ARE BUILT FOR LOVE. IN THE CORE OF EVERY HUMAN being there is a longing to love and be loved. The decision we make to love without limitations or conditions is the choice of clean love. The understanding of unconditional love is the lifelong journey. Humans want to put "ifs and buts" on love. Love can be withheld or cut off when conditions are not met. Conditional love is an imitation. Authentic love is unconditional. It's not about what someone else does or doesn't do in your life, it's about what your love does for others without limitations. Your love affects so many lives. It's the most treasured responsibility that you hold.

You wake up every morning and look in your mirror to see the image of yourself. It's time to look again. The image is the reflection of the Creator inside you. You are not a clone made from stem cells. You are an original. You and I are formed in the image of God. Love originated in God. At the core of who we are is love. Just like an apple holds its seeds in the core, the seed of love has been planted within us. Love is multiplied by planting its seeds in someone else.

Copying God

As children copy their fathers, you, as God's children are to copy Him. The look-at-me world we live in is vying for attention. I'm bigger, I'm stronger, I'm more beautiful, I'm more powerful, and the I-can-do-it-better-than-you mindset is now habitual. The ideas people carry determine how people respond to all situations. All ideas have consequences.

The truth is that the greatest among us is the servant to all. Whether a president or celebrity, an entrepreneur or farmer, Democrat or Republican, black or white, acknowledged or not, if there is good in you and me, it's from God. I am no expert, but I know The Expert and He is looking at the heart inside of us. In every challenge, failure, or disappointment, there is a hidden diamond in the rough. The eternal goal from God is to form a love in us that will not fail; it's the highest achievement in life. Your brilliance is underestimated by you. Discovering your identity of clean love spins the gem inside of you under the shine of His light. This reflection will capture the attention of others by His magnificent power of love inside of you and me.

The Mystery of Love

Mysteries are divine secrets. They baffle our understanding and things that can't be explained leave us in awe. After thousands of years of study, there are profound mysteries in every sphere of life that are still to be discovered. Love is that way. It keeps unfolding its mystery in our lives. There are layers and layers of this strongest force in the world yet to be uncovered.

Natural treasured pearls are formed as a parasite works its way into a clam or oyster. As a defense mechanism, a fluid forms and coats around the irritant. Year after year, layer upon layer of this coating are deposited around the parasite until a lustrous pearl is formed. Believe it or not, love is formed out of the parasite of sin in the heart of man. Year after year layers and layers of the truth of love cover the multitude of sins in the heart of man. Out of that covering come the pearls of love and faithfulness. This necklace of love is bound around the necks of people who have this written statement on the tablet of their hearts: "this life has been paid for by God's love." Why? Because God's love is natural.

What is natural about His love? It's as natural as any mother loving her child. It's as natural as any father taking responsibility and wanting to protect his children. It's as natural as any baby needing milk to survive. We are the heart of the matter to God and as His sons and daughters He wants us to succeed and prosper in everything good—especially love. I heard it said this way:

When you're at home in God and He's at home in you—that's real love. Simple, clean, and natural.

What Love Is and What Love Isn't

The most famous passage of scripture is quoted at weddings and funerals. Whether you believe or not, most of us have heard or seen these beautiful words. They can be found on prints at Home Goods, written on Hallmark cards and coffee cups, scripted in movies, or hanging on a wall in your house. They are on my refrigerator. Yet most people do not have these words written on their hearts because they have become common and ordinary. These words embody what love is and what love isn't.

Love is patient, love is kind. It does not envy, it does not boast, it is not proud. It does not dishonor others, it is not self-seeking, it is not easily angered, it keeps no record of wrongs. Love does not delight in evil, but rejoices with the truth. It always protects, always trusts, always hopes, always perseveres.

This passage is *the* master key to open the door of our hearts to clean love. It will unlock and unblock every troubled soul. It's the bridge builder that connects every relationship. There is no racial, social, economic, governmental, religious, or language barrier that this passage, when lived out, cannot break through.

My Dear Reader, there is one constant question I hope you will keep in mind as you turn each page of this book. The answer holds everything you believe about yourself, as well as the keys to unlock the vault in your heart. This vault holds hidden treasure and is at the core of who you are:

WHAT DOES "CLEAN LOVE" LOOK LIKE IN YOU?

Let's begin this journey together to find the answer.

CHAPTER 2

THE SIGNS

What's the Matter?

I AM NOT ASKING YOU TO ANSWER WHAT'S THE MATTER *with the world . . . with our government . . . with the pandemic . . . or with the way we think about race. . . .*

I'm asking you to face the real truth of *what's the matter in you?* I can answer that question for you by telling you— <u>*it's what you think about most.*</u>

> Watch your thoughts, for they become your words.
> Watch your words, for they become actions.
> Watch your actions, for they become your habits.
> Watch your habits, for they become character.
> Watch your character, for it becomes your destiny.

When something is wrong, it shows up in countless ways. The evidence includes bad habits and addictions that bring temporary false comfort to our lives. When something is wrong, our thoughts and speech change. Voices that cannot hold a tune are suddenly octaves higher and louder. Words fling out like casting a fishing line, but later we reel in wishing we could take back those toxic words. At the end of the line we are always caught in a snarl. Our character can change from the bride of Christ to the bride of Frankenstein.

In my coaching, the mantra I use most is: "Words lie and words tell the truth but 'BEHAVIOR NEVER EVER LIES'" (credits to Richard Flint). The skeleton in your closet needs burial because secret behaviors are never unseen by God.

The number one area that's hindered when something is wrong is faith. We begin to doubt the people we love, and we begin to doubt God. We resist the truth instead of resisting the lie. We slide down a slippery slope into an emotional black hole that has no light. Doubt has a progression, it moves quickly to despair, and despair to depression. The ancient wisdom of the book of Proverbs speaks of depression this way: *A man who isolates himself seeks his own desire: he rages against all wise judgment.* Isolation from God and people is never healthy.

God has a way of getting to the bottom of things because that is where all the sediment is. The great news is that He will get to the heart of the matter because you and I matter. At times, faith is just showing up. If you've purchased this book and are turning these pages, you have shown up. The time for change is now. A new season has started. Not every apple grows on the first day of apple season but it's still the season of fruit. Bearing anything in life takes breathing, pushing, blood, sweat, and tears. Embrace the process. We live in a "fast food mentality," *we want it now, and we want it our way.* God does not bend the rules. His only three answers to all our questions are yes, no, and wait. You have shown up, and you have begun the process of clean love, let this book wash your heart. Keep reading. . . .

Indicator Lights

Indicator lights tell us that something needs to be checked. When something is wrong with your car the indicator light comes on your dashboard telling you to check the engine, you need oil, or your gas is low. If you ignore the indicators your car will break down. Your emotions are your indicator lights. If gone unchecked, out of control emotions will break you down. Think about what triggers you. Not "who" triggers you, *"what"* triggers you. Your trigger is like a switch button that you wear on your mind. When pushed, triggers bring back the emotions of a bad memory or trauma. There is no forewarning of flipping the switch, it happens in a split second. The result ends with some sort of flare up emotionally. Identifying triggers helps overcome them. The only way someone can push your buttons is if you have buttons to push.

When my Mom passed away, we had the task of cleaning out her home. Like many older people my mom had a hard time throwing things away. Her closet was full of vintage clothing. As I was going through her clothes, I noticed many had unique buttons. I began to take the buttons off of her clothes with a creative idea in mind. I glued the buttons on Styrofoam cones shaped like Christmas trees. I gave them as gifts to friends and family as a memorial of my Mom.

Not all buttons are beautiful. Don't wait until you die for your negative buttons to come off.

To identify them, recognize when your thoughts tell you things like:

She/He drives me crazy. . . . I can't take this anymore. . . . I don't know. . . . I'm worried. . . . Nobody cares. . . . I'm confused. . . . I'm not loved. . . . The blinking indicator light also goes on when you have conflicting thoughts, holding two opinions at the same time. When you know for certain your "yes" means "yes" and your "no" is definitely "no," your indicator light of out-of-control emotions will shut off. When you replace the toxic thought life with truth from God, your trigger button will disappear. An ounce of prevention is definitely worth a pound of cure.

The Stop Sign of Deception

Deceptions always hold a little bit of truth. The key is to recognize them. It's only when you do that you will stop the power deception holds over you. A stop sign means STOP! It doesn't mean roll through it or run it or coast.

It means STOP.

Stop—self-condemnation.
Stop—negative talk.
Stop—living in the past.
Stop—fear, fret, and worry.

The following story will explain deception. It is an old story about a snake in your basement. Yes, this is **your** story.

Imagine that you need something from your basement. When you flip the light at the top of your stairs, the bulb blows out. In the dim light, you fumble your way down the stairs to get what you need. Suddenly, in the corner of the room, you see a large snake. *"Oh My God!"* is your first thought before you run out of the basement in fear and panic and try to find someone who can help you get the snake out. Your friend comes and brings his flashlight. He asks you, "Where did you see the snake?" You point to the corner of the room where you saw the snake. Your friend laughs and says, "Look, that's not a snake, it's a coiled-up hose!" Again, your *"Oh My God"* comes. You are relieved now and laughing along with your friend.

Minutes before, everything in you reacted in fret, fear, and worry because your truth was that a real snake was in your basement. It felt like a snake, it looked like a snake, it must be a snake. When the light shined on it, you found out it really wasn't a snake at all, just a coiled-up hose.

This is how we get deceived about ourselves and life. It looks like it, it feels like it, so it must be it. We believe these impure deceptions as truth and get stuck in life. When we allow God's light to shine on the deceptions in the basement of our hearts, our perceptions change. We understand things on a deeper level, gain inner security, and eradicate fears.

Warning Signals

The voice you want to ignore is the voice you should listen to. On a beautiful fall Friday morning four years ago, I got up knowing I had a hectic schedule ahead of me. I wanted to get some errands done early. I went to the bank at 9 a.m. I knew some of the tellers by name, as I have been banking there for years. That morning I happened to be the only customer in the bank. There was a new manager who introduced herself and greeted me warmly and we began to chat. As our conversation continued, I didn't want to be rude—but I had to go. The voice in my mind said *"you're in a traffic jam."* In coaching I use that statement all the time to explain to people that when you're in a traffic jam in life, don't complain. God may be sparing you from an accident. When I heard it in my mind, I paid attention. So instead of rushing, I released my rush and engaged in the conversation. Within a few minutes, armed and masked bank robbers entered and yelled, "Hands up!" My hands went up but my knees went down and I hit the floor. Instinctively I knew the only thing I could do was pray. It was as if God put His fingers in my ears, everything was muffled, I closed my eyes and focused on praying. "Don't let the gun go off . . . protection . . . keep everybody safe."

It all happened really fast. The robbers ran out of the bank. The bank went on lockdown and the next thing I heard were instructions from the manager to the tellers, not to speak but to write down the descriptions of the robbers. No gun was fired and no one was injured. As these men ran out of the bank, they knocked over a little old lady who was entering the bank. Within minutes, there were many police officers and detectives taking statements. The little old lady testified that she saw a car running as she was walking through the parking lot to enter the bank. She thought to herself "Who leaves their car running in this day and age?" That car was their car, which was parked next to my car. If I had left the bank in my rush—who knows? I may have encountered them in the parking lot. God kept me safer in the bank. That voice in my head "you're in a traffic jam" was His voice. I could have ignored it and who knows? God knows.

Months later I was called by the FBI to come and give a statement. The robbers had been caught and they were interviewing everybody who was at the scene that day. I was asked to recount every detail that I could remember about that morning. I was glad to help but as I sat with three FBI Agents at the interview, I asked them if they knew the Holy Spirit? They looked at me strangely. I told them He is part of the story, because He warned me not to leave the bank. This is the same story that I am telling you. Warning signals come from Him. Pay attention to His voice as it often comes in ways we don't expect.

CHAPTER 3

TRANSITION TRIPS

YOU ARE NOW GOING ON A TRIP. THIS ISN'T JUST ANY TRIP. It's a *transition trip*. Transition trips are not beach vacations. They are not weekend breaks, road trips, visits with friends or relatives, nor are they business travel. Transition trips in life take us to places we never dreamed we would go and we would never willingly choose. These trips have no tickets, no preplanning, and no packing required. When you embark, you have no expectations about weather and no anticipation or excitement. This trip happens and unfolds through the trials of life.

Life happens in minutes and moments, but when we are on a transition trip, it always leaves us begging one question . . . *"How long until this is over?"* Only He knows the answer; it is never revealed to us in advance. It's as long as it takes to create something beautiful in us because when the trip is over treasure will be found on the inside.

When life takes a definite turn, we board the airplane of suspense to the unknown. A fear of flying has no choice on this trip, for we must board the plane. Our sense of control is completely out of our control. We buckle up in fear, hold on, and pray as turbulence and pressure become a constant. Unexpected crisis, tragedies, life-altering situations, didn't-see-that-coming moments make up the transition trips of life. Whether it's marriage, health, money, relationships, death, breakups, failures, divorce, job loss, getting older, losing everything . . . no one escapes transition trips. Transition trips are unforgettable and the exact time and date become engraved in our memories forever.

On March 3rd, 2020 at 12:30 a.m., Nashville, Tennessee was devastated by an F3 tornado that tore through the heart and soul of Germantown, the area of the city where our daughter, Lindsay, lived. That same evening in Connecticut, Dan and I were hosting our regular Monday night prayer meeting which we have held for twenty-five years. We wrapped up around 10 p.m. and a few friends stayed on to enjoy food and fellowship. Around midnight, I announced to our friends that we needed to adjourn, but before we did, I felt compelled to pray for protection for our children. I had no idea a tornado was about to hit our daughter's apartment building. God has a way of prompting us to pray. Sometimes we follow the prompt and sometimes we don't. I am so thankful I paid attention to His prompt that night.

In a moment, on that night in March, Lindsay began her transition trip. She awoke to the sound of heavy rain and strong winds rattling the large picture window next to her bed. She immediately decided to go check on her dog. Within two seconds of closing her bedroom door behind her, the picture window next to her bed blew up. Shards of glass crashed all over her bed where just seconds before she had been sleeping. Water began streaming through the ceiling. The chaos of the next few minutes found her wandering through the dark streets. She was walking through downed wires and the chaotic aftermath to get to safety. This was the beginning of her life being displaced. What to do next?

When flying blind, a pilot must rely on the instrument panel to navigate successfully without visual cues. Similarly, when you can't see ahead because of the transition of trials, you will want to rely on your *gut instruments*. Your gut *is* your inner compass because it's where the Holy Spirit lives inside of you. He is your power source of love and courage. But when your inner compass is off, it affects the course of actions and direction you will take. It is known that if a pilot is just one degree off course, an airplane will veer ninety-two feet away from it's destination for every mile it flies. For your inner compass to keep you on course, you'll need gut courage to operate out of the internal truth that He shares with you. Worry will only steer you incorrectly through life and it will prevent you from hearing the right message. Difficulty uses *courage* as its indicator. Without courage you will move further toward confusion.

When your inside parts are set on worry, your health is affected with chronic unbalanced emotions. This difficulty craves and clings to unclean thinking causing the bacteria of toxic negative emotions to surface. You no longer can absorb the truth. Thoughts are captive in a revolving door of lies that you believe about yourself and are a precursor to speech *dis-ease*. Your sleepless nights go on and your mood changes. Good judgment becomes impaired. As poor behavior manifests, it's difficult to get back on course.

When we go through turbulence, we wait until the plane steadies to catch our breath. Yes, we have to catch it, because we lost it.

In working with people, I have heard many sad and difficult stories, but I have watched God use time as a healer. The transition of trials holds a destination that eventually works for our good. The most amazing thing about Lindsay's transition trip was that the day before the tornado, she had told her Dad, "Something has to change; I want to get out of this lease. God has to do something."

After the tornado hit Lindsay's apartment, more difficulty came (adding insult to injury) as COVID-19 began to spread in the United States. Lindsay found herself living in a short stay hotel in Nashville with her dog and she was struggling to see where her future was heading.

In order to set things back on track, we often must come back to center. I kept feeling like Lindsay should come home to Connecticut. Flights were difficult to find because of COVID, and traveling with a 55-pound boxer bulldog made it exceedingly difficult. She caught one of the last planes traveling north only to get twenty minutes away from Westchester Airport and have to turn back to Atlanta because they closed the airport. To make a long story short, she and her dog, Blue, finally arrived after twenty-two hours of travel from Nashville to New York.

Love begins at home. It is where the heart is. Being home provides a time to heal, laugh, and cry. It's the center of love in family life. We cherished every moment Lindsay was home with us, but her destiny was to be fulfilled and it wasn't in Connecticut. She began making plans in her heart, but we all know it's God who directs our steps. The domino effect would begin for the next part of her life's journey in the form of a text message from a former client, which opened the door to a beautiful new place in Nashville. I am here now in her space in Tennessee as an eyewitness that only God could have done this, because I know He works everything out for good for those who love Him and are called according to his purpose.

The Miracle of Transformation

The outcome of your transition trip will end in transformation. There will be change, improvement, growth, development, and freedom.

Consider the butterfly. . . . A butterfly's story starts when a caterpillar is hatched from an egg and eats its way through its short life until one day the caterpillar stops eating, hangs upside down from a twig, and spins itself a cocoon. Inside this tight spot, the caterpillar radically transforms its body, eventually emerging as a butterfly.

Scientists have learned that butterfly wings are made up of living cells. They are actually alive. The wings help regulate temperature and keep the butterfly from overheating in the sun. They have discovered a *"wing heart"* that beats a few dozen times per minute to facilitate blood flow. The butterfly's struggle to get out of the cocoon is what gives it the strength to fly. The struggle is very real, and without it there can be no freedom. Butterflies fly freely. It is well known that Monarch butterflies travel up to 3000 miles across the open waters of the ocean and wait for the wind to help them across during their annual migration. They use the position of the sun to lead them and have a magnetic compass that gives them the sense of direction.

The test of your struggle reveals your weakness and proves your strength. Out of the ashes of trials arise great blessings. It's not the place you end up, *it's the heart you end up with*. In your transition trip, if you find God, you will find your courage. Courage affects everyone around you. The outcome of love throughout the journey gives you courage to become the best version of yourself. Give Him your love in the darkest place in your life and you will find your *"winged heart"* passionately beating and you will soar. . . . Use the wind of His Spirit and look to His Son. When pain finishes its work, something beautiful emerges. You wouldn't change it for the world.

Consider it pure joy, my brothers and sisters, whenever you face trials of many kinds, because you know that the testing of your faith produces perseverance. Let perseverance finish its work so that you may be mature and complete, not lacking anything.

CHAPTER 4

THE SOURCE AND STEPS: ESSENTIALS FOR CLEAN LOVE

A SOURCE IS A PLACE WHERE SOMETHING BEGINS, THE point of origin where something springs into being—a person, place, or thing from which something comes or can be obtained. A well is dug because there is a water source under the ground beneath it. Solar energy comes from the source of the sun. Doctors look at X-rays for the source of an illness. And I look to God as the source for this writing. He is the *Great Physician*—the only one who can clean our hearts, heal us, and return us to the authentic, original image of how we are designed to live out this amazing gift of life we are given.

Out of a man's mouth comes from what's within his heart.

The confusion of different opinions attempts to lure us away from the true source of hope and truth. But these different opinions are merely examples of how we look to the wrong source. When we look to people to have our expectations fulfilled, the answers fall short and we end up holding others hostage by their words. We deceive ourselves by trying to bend to the whim of culture or preferences. Trying to fix an inward problem with an outward solution never works. Again, God does not look at outward appearances; He looks at the heart. Finding wisdom, taking steps, and using the essentials He gave us is His ordered process. The process is one step at a time.

Listening to Wisdom's Counsel

Where is wisdom? Is there a place I can go to get understanding? Not a person on earth grasps how much value wisdom has; heaven touching earth is magnificent. God is the only one who can direct us to wisdom; He has it in its destiny place. He knows every detail of the earth. He sees everything below heaven. He commanded everything to line up right and in order so that seasons could do their job. He stared at wisdom. It was perfect for every human being. He revealed its secret: **Fear God** *that is what wisdom is and understanding makes an about face from evil.*

Step 1: Ready, Willing, and Able

If you're ready and willing, you will be able. Ready or not, life is full of changes. Willingness sustains us through the changes. Opening allows light. The first step in being willing is accepting that He is our Source. It is being open to His guidance and the leading of His Spirit. It's hard for me to believe that you may not believe that. But I realize some of you may be in a place where you say: I don't believe in God. That is your choice. But it will never change the fact that *He believes in you.*

This first step is the hardest because it's where your

commitment lives. Commitment to anything takes obedience, discipline, hard work, reassurance, accountability, strategy, faith, tenacity, blood, sweat, and tears. When you are committed, your character is revealed. Find a mentor, a counselor, a coach, a friend, a person who will push you forward, tell you the truth, give you wise council, hold you accountable, stretch your thinking and help you flourish.

Step 2: Wake Up Your Senses

Wake up, Oh sleeper

You and I have six senses. Five of them are natural. The sixth is our prophetic sense. Our senses are the gates in our bodies and they include the eye gate, the ear gate, the mouth gate, the nose gate, the sex gate, and the spiritual gate. When the gates are violated, fear and torment will manifest within us. We need to protect the gates from what we see with our eyes, which can cause terror within us. We need to protect what we hear with our ears, because words can take us to prison in our own minds. We need to protect what we take in through our nose and mouth, because pollution and gluttony of any kind can poison the body. And we need to protect from dishonoring the sex gate, which can spread the sins of what others carry into ourselves.

We have all had a wilderness experience or a time of rebellion. I remember mine well. I was going to do it my way—and I did. I personally know what it's like to rebel in sexual promiscuity, and I paid the price of that sin with years of struggle and torment, with panic, guilt, and shame. Shame haunts, and I was haunted every day for years. Even through counseling I struggled to accept that I could be forgiven. God will go to any length to bring His unquestionable love and forgiveness to us. Years later, my son was born on the anniversary of the date of the biggest regret of my life, because God wanted to show me His love forgives. His love has no boundaries. My time of haunting ended.

If I could do it all over again, *believe me*, I would do things differently. Who wouldn't? We don't get a chance to go back, but we do get a new day today. Today is the only day we have right now. Living fully in today is vital and the most important thing about today is to hear His voice. Living in regret, shame, and the past will keep you right there—in the past.

A hardened heart keeps us from hearing; it keeps us "dull in senses." *Their minds are dull and slow to perceive, their ears are plugged and are hard of hearing, and yet they have deliberately shut their eyes to the truth. Otherwise they would open their eyes to see, and open their ears to hear, and open their minds to understand. Then they would turn to me and let me instantly heal them.*

I remember being in a hotel in Canada. I was sound asleep when at 3:00 a.m. the fire alarm went off. Immediately, healthy fear awakened my senses to high alert. When your antenna goes up you can catch the frequency and get out of harm's way. I had to try to see, smell, and hear what was happening and I remember trying to find the light switch in the midst of panic. When the internal alarm is going off inside of us, we need to pay attention and the antenna of our senses need to be on high alert. God uses the fire of our circumstances to wake us up. *Naivety keeps us sleeping in the dark* while there is a raging fire burning. Fire either destroys or purifies. Maturity understands what healthy fear is, and makes intentional choices to face the issues head on in order to be purified. The more purified we are, the more freedom we receive.

Step 3: Breathe

But it is the spirit in a person, the breath of the Almighty that gives them understanding.

Our bodies are made in such an amazing way. Right now, while you are reading this, you are breathing. You are not focusing on it. Breathing is an automatic bodily function, but *deliberate breathing* is intentional and beneficial to the body, mind, and spirit. Taking ten deep breaths decreases stress, relieves pain, stimulates the lymphatic system, improves immunity, increases energy, lowers blood pressure, improves digestion, and helps support and correct posture and more.

During this reading process it is so important for you to be intentional about breathing. The challenge is to take your deep breaths every day. It is so simple, free, and easy that we can easily miss it. Breathe deliberately and intentionally with the understanding that the air you take in and out of your lungs belongs to God. As you breathe, receive.

Take a deep breath.

CHAPTER 5

WHY DO YOU FEAR LOVE?

Kissing a Pit Bull

I WAS ALWAYS TOLD THAT PIT BULLS CAN KILL YOU.

I lived on a farm growing up and throughout my whole life I have always owned dogs. I love dogs but when it comes to pit bulls, I would gladly run a mile in the other direction. At one point, we lived in a home where our neighbors had a pit bull and I would not let my children go outside to play when the dog was out, even on a leash. I never dreamed that my daughter would own a breed of dog connected to a pit. Blue, who is now fifty-five pounds strong, was the five-pound runt of a boxer bulldog litter. I was so upset when Lindsay chose this dog to adopt as her own. I had to face my fear of pit bulls or risk not seeing my daughter. When she arrived here with Blue for her month-long stay, my heart rate went up and so did my prayers because of the dog. I had to get my fear sorted out. I had no choice but to break years of negative conditioning fearing that this dog would hurt me. I got to know Blue by spending time with her. She longed for a morning scratch and every morning it became our bonding time, sometimes lasting thirty minutes. She would lay belly-up and wait for me to scratch her body and love on her. If I stopped, she would relentlessly push on me for more. This didn't happen with everybody; it was only with me. The scratch time was our little thing and it began to melt my fears.

A month after Lindsay and Blue left, I arrived in Tennessee. Blue went crazy when she saw me—kissing, licking, and loving me. Courage is the ability to do something that frightens you. It's not a lack of fear rather it's the ability to face it. Blue loves to be loved. I never thought I would love the kisses of this dog. God used Blue to break a curse.

Some fears have their origin in a generational curse. Generational curses come down from your family line. My mom was so great in so many ways but she struggled with worry and fear her whole life. Always worrying about "what if" and I grew up living very nervous because of it. *What if this happens?* My Mom's *"what ifs"* almost never happened. I was an anxious kid, an anxious teenager, and an anxious young adult. What was ingrained in my brain was the possibility of disaster happening in all kinds of situations in my life. When I got older, I used to joke and say my Mom could make a tranquilizer nervous. Generational curses come through spoken words and actions often from people in our own family. Those curses were never birthed out of love but were passed to us from a "spirit of fear."

Just as Blue thrived when I loved on her, pitbull-personality people thrive when love exists. Impossible becomes nothing. The generational curses we carry, caused by the actions and words of people, take time to heal. Can they be broken? Of course! Face your fears—spend time with what you fear, or who you fear, or where you fear. Ask yourself why you fear. And when you spell love, spell it with faith: R-I-S-K. God is always ready to help us break through. Something has to break in order for breakthrough to happen.

Loneliness Fears

There are times in life when you may have felt your pain is invisible and ignored by the ones around you. Loneliness feels unpleasant. It begs for relief of pain. It hides and masks its brokenness and fills a vortex of "alone" with antidotes of all kinds. There are many people who can be in a crowded room and still feel very lonely. The longing for companionship—to have someone to be by our side through life's thick-and-thin episodes and to share memories and miles of life with—is a heart's desire. God put that desire in the heart of humans.

When there are repeated disappointments, dreams may get abandoned. Often people who are chronically lonely fall into depression, addiction, and even suicidal thoughts. One of the biggest things loneliness does is project wrong beliefs about the future. If this is you, you don't need to be brainwashed—you need to be heart washed. The only enemy of your future is fear.

Your identity is not what you think! If you misidentify yourself, you will be misdirected. Life is a total of all decisions, choices, and corresponding actions. Loneliness will tell you there must be something wrong with you. It destroys you from the inside out. The times of your life of the greatest brokenness can be the times of the greatest value and validation. These times carry a huge degree of humility. Making the step of mentorship will bring direction, encouragement, and affirmation.

Use your time to get healthy—emotionally, physically, and spiritually—whatever that looks like for you. The step in the direction of accountability is always the right step. Every open door is an opportunity, and your yes to those doors are critical. Even if there is a detour or delay your faith to make the steps will take you where God wants you to go. You will find others who need your love.

Faith Versus Fear

In a boxing ring, only two things happen—either you throw a punch or you defend yourself from one. The only good fight in life is the fight of faith. The tests come every day as faith and fear box each other; one will overcome the other. Without faith we cannot please God; without fear we cannot please evil. All throughout life there are tests—relationships tests, honor tests, respect tests, integrity tests, character tests, and giving tests.

In 2009 I was at a conference in Sioux Falls, South Dakota. During one of the sessions, a pastor from Los Angeles named Althea Sims was speaking. I had never met her until that day. She shared her courageous testimony about how her whole life changed in a day: "*On March 26, 2000, my family and I experienced the greatest challenge of our lives. My 51-year-old husband, who was a bi-vocational pastor, suffered a massive stroke right before my eyes. Our lives were changed forever . . . home, marriage, ministry, vocation, and finances. Three months after the stroke, my husband's employer went belly-up, which caused us to lose his income, our medical insurance coverage, and retirement. The Lord miraculously sustained us through the years. However, by 2009, we found ourselves facing the loss of our home. I pressed my way to attend a conference with very little funds to my name."*

After Althea spoke there was an offering taken for her and her family. I closed my eyes and prayed to ask the Lord how much I should give. What I heard in my spirit, shook me. I prayed again, and again I heard the same number. "But God, this will wipe out our savings, emergency fund, and money toward a college fund." It was everything we had saved in the bank. I struggled with the thought of that. I have learned in my experience with God that immediate obedience to His voice is real faith. I gave out of faith. In faith, I knew it was God's money. But fear and faith began to box. Fear isn't a funny thing; it comes on you in waves when you least expect it. I had waves and waves of fear hit me. I had never done anything like this before and truly I was terrified about the decision, questioning myself. It wasn't until I spoke to my husband and he asked me one question, "Did you hear from God? "Yes," was my answer . . . and he said, "Send the check." My fear ended.

This battle for love's victory is won by doing what you can, when you can, while you can. God so loved; He gave. Faith will move the mountain of fear. I am friends with Althea to this very day. I have visited her and Reggie (her husband), in the wheelchair-accessible house where they had lived for many years. A domino effect of miracles hap-pened. *God did that.*

CHAPTER 6

TODAY IS THE ONLY DAY YOU HAVE TO LOVE

WE ARE BUSY PEOPLE, BUSY THINKING. THE LATEST STATIS-
tics say that the human mind thinks about fifty thousand
thoughts per day, which means about twenty-one hundred thoughts per hour. *Of those, 80 percent are negative
and 95 percent are repetitive.*

As a man thinks, so he is.

There are times that real rest is needed. The sit-down-
and-listen opportunities are daily but most of us are too
busy to seize them. Life offers two kinds of rest—willing
rest or forced rest.

One day, while walking on a beautiful trail in the
woods, I was busy confessing scripture. I was determined
to get my prayer walk done (multitasking is a gift that
women do best). I spoke aloud this passage, "*Today is the
day the Lord has made. I will rejoice and be glad in it.*" I was
abruptly interrupted. It was then that I heard an internal
voice that said, "*STOP!*"

I thought, "Excuse me?"

Again, I heard "*STOP!*" . . . I sensed that God was asking me how I was going to rejoice in this day? My answer
came quickly: "I'm going to pray, be thankful, do something nice for someone." . . . But again, I heard, "*STOP!*"
I immediately knew it was time to sit down and listen. I

found a big rock and quieted myself, waiting to hear the voice I longed to hear. In just a few moments I heard a bird singing its heart out and the sound of the river below the trail that was bubbling like a hot tub.

That bird was probably singing the whole time I was confessing scripture, but I was too busy hearing myself to hear this bird. The river below the trail was bubbling with the sound of "many waters" it was right under my ears, close enough for comfort, but my agenda overtook my hearing. I could now see incredible streams of light in the woods. I hadn't noticed them during my walk because I was busy "human doing." I could feel the fresh air and I could smell the fragrance of the woods. I almost missed the peace and solace of God's creation that day. Life is a series of moments and missing moments happen fast. I understood while sitting on that rock that I was now sitting at God's table and He had my full attention. *He **makes me** lie down in green pastures and leads me beside still waters. . . .*

Agree with Love: Clink Your Glass

While sitting on that rock, in a flash I remembered a scene from my childhood: I grew up in a big, loud, Italian family and our supper table resounded with emotional volcanic eruptions of argument or laughter. My family was passionate about whatever was being discussed. Our dinner table always included old and new friends as my parents had the gift of hospitality. Wine was poured at every supper. Food was authentic Italian.

My favorite part of the meal, before chaos exploded,

was always the toast. I couldn't wait to hold my little milk glass up to clink the wine glasses as my father would say in Italian *Alla Salute* ("To Health"). The clink of the glasses was that *moment of agreement* by everyone at the table before the invisible bell would sound for the supper table to become a boxing ring. The debates of life would begin over a great meal.

The clink of glasses made me happy, it paused crazy, it was a moment of joy, it was honoring, it created unity, and that clink was an *agreement of love* in spite of the chaos. Again, the inside whisper came, *it is only when you are at My table and you agree with My Word and My Spirit that you can fully rejoice and be glad in this day.* Lip service won't allow you to celebrate this day. The day needs to be found by your spirit becoming alive to His Spirit, in agreement. Toasting with God.

CHAPTER 7

THE BLOCKAGES OF LOVE

Calluses

For this people's heart has grown callous, their ears are dull of hearing, and they have closed their eyes; or else perhaps they might perceive with their eyes, hear with their ears, understand with their heart, and would turn again and I would heal them.

Calluses don't form overnight, they form over time. We go to bed with the cares of life and we wake up with the cares of life. We go to bed angry and we wake up angry. We go to bed with anxiety and we wake up with anxiety. It is important to know that calluses become blockages and blockages cause an unclean heart. Blockages in the physical heart provide an analogy to explain spiritual and emotional blockages. . . .

Years ago, my husband Dan had a heart attack. Dan is a magnificent man, a wonderful husband, father, and friend. He is a person who lives life happy. He is a creative and hardworking man who loves God, his family, and his country with his whole heart. He is a man of prayer. He is very fit, and has spent the mornings of the last thirty-eight years of our marriage, first with God, and then at the gym at 6:00 a.m. Our kids call him Superman. What happened on the day of his sixtieth birthday was God's birthday gift to him.

As a third-generation stonemason, he was on a job when he experienced pain in his chest. Dismissing it as, "maybe I pulled a muscle," he kept working. But the persistence of pain did not subside so he quit early and came home.

I had been at the grocery store, and on my way home I was delighted to see his number come up on my phone. I greeted him with an excited "Happy Birthday!" but the voice that I heard on the other end was serious. Dan said, "Gene, I think I'm having a heart attack."

I reassured him that I'd be home in minutes, hung up, and called 911. I drove record speed while begging God to spare his life and arrived home to find Dan sitting in a chair, gray in color. He told me not to touch him because he was in such great pain. The ambulance arrived (I pause to say thank you to our First Responders, Police, and Firemen who are true heroes), and Dan was rushed to the hospital where it was confirmed that he was having a heart attack. Within minutes, doctors whisked him to the OR to perform an angioplasty. Dan was awake during the procedure and asked repeatedly to breathe as the doctor unclogged and removed the blockages in his heart. An hour later, after receiving four stents, he was in recovery eating a cheeseburger and cheesecake! He now has a second chance at life and is grateful for God's most amazing sixtieth birthday gift.

Just as Dan received God's gift of life through a physical angioplasty, you can receive a spiritual and emotional angioplasty to release the blockages that hinder you from living a life of clean love. Instead of just surviving life, the possibilities are endless to live a thriving life. As you *receive freedom*, you will be released from being an enabler, from being a victim, from rejection, from living in the past, and from feeding unhealthy fears that hold you captive in anger, hurt, and offense. Without freedom, blockages such as these cause you to live life with hidden self-biases and deceptions—it's like a heart attack waiting to happen. Just like an angioplasty is used to widen narrowed or obstructed arteries so blood can flow unhindered; allowing your eyes, heart, and mind to be open to change will change you. It's time for the reset in your heart and life. This emotional and spiritual angioplasty is the process that removes the hidden callouses and blockages. All it takes is a willingness to look on the inside, to go through the process, and to be open to God.

Hindsight

The truth is that hindsight is only 20/20. Looking back, Dan was having headaches and fatigue in the weeks leading up to the heart attack. Additionally, he was eating Tylenol like candy. He ignored these symptoms thinking they were merely signs of aging. Dan had no idea the heart attack was coming because he dismissed the warning signs. He didn't know he had blockages and by ignoring symptoms, fear and self-diagnosis stopped him from preventative measures.

Just like Dan had signs of an impending heart attack in

the physical world, we have spiritual and emotional warning signs that we may not be able to see clearly by ourselves. Deep down, we know there is something wrong, but fear and self-diagnoses cause us to mask up, make excuses, shift blame, and ignore symptoms. Yet, we are quick to point out the things we see in others, while we ignore the problems inside of us. Ignoring only works for so long before something surfaces.

Dan received nitroglycerin during his angioplasty, which alleviated the pain by relaxing the muscles in the walls of the heart causing them to dilate. Dan was awake during the procedure and the doctor told him to take a deep breath each time a blockage was being removed. I believe that as you read the next chapters of this book, slowly blockages will be removed, just breathe.

CHAPTER 8

THE CLEAN HEART CHECK

Love is *patient*, love is *kind*. It does not *envy*,
it does not *boast*, it is not *proud*. It does not *dishonor*
others, it is not *self-seeking*, it is not easily *angered*, it
keeps no record of *wrongs*. Love does not delight in
evil, but *rejoices* with the truth. It always *protects*,
always *trusts*, always *hopes*, always *perseveres*.

ONE OF THE TOOLS I KEEP IN MY COACHING TOOLBOX IS
something I call "The Clean Heart Check." Answering
the questions below will allow you to evaluate the state of
your own heart.

*Create in me a clean heart, O God; and renew a right
spirit within me.* This is not a suggestion but rather an
understanding that the heart of man is dirty and needs
cleaning. Somehow there are people of faith who believe
this applies to others, but this is needed for everyone.

The following ten questions reveal some of what you
really believe about yourself—much like an ultrasound
exposing deeper hidden issues of your heart.

1. Are you patient? (How you drive answers that.)
2. Are you kind?
3. Do you want what someone else has?
4. Do you think you are valued?

5. Are you honorable/do you keep your word?
6. Are you easily offended/are you angry?
7. Do you hold unforgiveness?
8. Is money a source of worry?
9. Do you blame others or make excuses?
10. Are you fearful on a regular basis?

There is one more question but it's not one for you to answer. It's a question that you ask and, in fact, it is the number one question of the human heart. It's been asked by every human being since the beginning of time. It is threaded throughout every book of the Bible. You and I ask this question consciously or subconsciously every day. In coaching, many people have told me what they believe the question is: Why am I here? What's my purpose? Or, does God love me? Those are probably in the top five, but the question of the human heart is . . .

How Long?

We start out as kids in the backseat of a car asking, "How long till we get there?" *How long?* is included in every person's yearning to know when something will occur or when something will end.

How long till I get a job?
How long till I get married?
How long until I live on my own?
How long till we eat?
How long until I get better?
How long will this last?

Etc. etc. etc.

The answer to your "How long?" and mine is this: *As long as it takes.*

Long-suffering births patience in us. We hear the word "suffering" and we want to run in the opposite direction. God uses our long-suffering as a muscle builder to our faith. Humanity is suffering in pain, some of the pain is necessary and some of the pain is unnecessary. It's interesting that one of the root meanings of long-suffering is to *take a deep breath.*

Patience

Patience is the ability to endure under pressure.

The thing that must be pruned back in us is our impatience. I went to a vineyard in Connecticut and spoke with the owner. I asked him to tell me about the pruning process. He shared with me that pruning back the vines is done during the dormant season. Because of this, the plant never feels the cutting off process. In the push-button culture that we live in, patience has waned. Frustration leads to exaggeration and people are out of the fuel of right thinking that drives patience. We lose patience within ourselves. This happens when we are double-minded (having conflicting thoughts, or holding two opinions at the same time), and leads us to waver in the valley of decision. What we really need is to be intentional in decision-making. *Let your yes be yes and your no be no.* "No" is a complete sentence. Your patience will thrive when you stop living in a gray area. This is the area that says, "I don't know."

All of life we are dealing with people. Our patience with the imperfections of others is fully realized in remembering that people around us have to deal with the imperfections in us. Many of us have heard of "the patience of Job" because of his endurance through great suffering and loss. Yet he emerged from darkness with his steps bathed in butter and cream. Victory came. God has a pruning process and it's not meant to hurt us; it's meant to flourish us.

Love is patient. Take a deep breath.

Kindness

Kindness is the activity of doing good.

Most of us would consider ourselves to be kind people. But there is a kindness that is extraordinary, unusual, and it sets us apart. We know we have this kind of kindness when we give what we treasure most. It could be our time, our talent, our money, our wisdom or a valuable material item that we love. It's the kind of kindness that costs us something.

The Old Testament is filled with amazing stories and there is one about a temple being built. On this temple pillars were erected that were twenty-seven feet tall—taller than any man. On the top of the pillars, craftsmen who were "filled with wisdom and understanding" sculpted beautiful lilies. These *Lily works* of kindness were done unto God because He was the only one who could see them.

When kindness becomes part of our identity people around us notice. *Kindness makes a man attractive.* When we walk in the identity of kindness, it transforms the lives of others. When you understand that identity you know who you are and you know who God is; everything around begins to line up.

Love is kind. Take a deep breath.

Love Gives, Lust Takes

Envy wants what someone else has, and jealously hates what someone else has.

The grass only appears greener; it's still just grass. Comparing is a slippery slope that will always take you deep into despair. The truth is, you and I are uniquely and wonderfully made. This means there is only one you and only one me.

Here lies the plague. It's the plague of self-importance; The "I-Me" pandemic.

Look at me. . . .
Look who I am with. . . .
Look where I'm at. . . .
Look what I'm doing. . . .
Look at what I'm eating. . . .
Look at what I have.

Selfie, the ultimate form of self, selfish, self-righteous, point to self. There is a vacuum of self that we have all gotten sucked into. *Let him deny himself, and take up his cross daily, and follow me.*

The battle of "Self" that we will fight our entire lives has three major strongholds. These three areas cannot only be conquered once, they need constant vigil. Our combat boots of peace need to be securely tied and we need to be armed and ready at a moment's notice to overcome these three invisible enemies.

The lust of the flesh says this: *I've had a bad day; you don't know what I've been through. I deserve my comfort.* Whether it's potato chips or pot, hoarding or heroin, the flesh needs temporary comfort to satisfy itself from some type of anguish or pain.

The lust of the eyes says this: *I see it and I want it. It doesn't matter if I can afford it. It doesn't matter if it belongs to my neighbor. It doesn't matter if I have to steal it to get it. I am going to have it.*

The pride of life says this: *I'm going to do it my way. Speak to the hand. I don't care. I know better than God.* Can you count how many times in your life you have said these three words: "I don't care"? Those three words coming from your mouth are a declaration that someone else's viewpoint is as good as garbage. Those three words throw people away, those three words dishonor and devalue, yet those three words are the three words that God never says.

Love does not envy or boast, it's not proud, it's not self-seeking. Take a deep breath.

Incessant Words and Dishonor

To repeat a matter separates good old friends.

Gossip is a blockage and the church gets away with it by deceptively whispering: *let me tell you so we can pray about it.* Troublemakers start fights and gossip breaks up friendships.

All of my life I have ridden horses. I grew up on a farm and learned to ride at a young age. I know what it's like to have a thousand-pound animal underneath my behind. The freedom to know I was safe from injury from this magnificent powerful animal was because of the bit in its mouth. If I pull back on the reins, the horse stops. A bit keeps a horse in check. Its mouth is the most sensitive part of its body and that small bit controls the whole animal.

Where there are many words sin is not absent. Many of us need a bit. What rolls off our tongues in accusations, opinion, insults, humiliations, and rejection puts others to shame—words that dishonor. Dishonor is a fire that is set by hell and it spreads out of control and causes great destruction.

Love does not dishonor others. Take a deep breath.

Break the Record

Anger is a human emotion, but when you play an offense over and over you get into plague mentality. Anything that plagues you, is a plague.

I coached a dear lady who had a reason to be angry. She was raped multiple times by a family member when she was young. This resulted in a life of torment. She told me she was an angry teenager, an angry young adult, an angry wife, and an angry mother. When she least expected it, uncontrollable rage would manifest from her. She had tried to resolve this with years of therapies of all kinds and eventually found her way to a church and to God. Her process wasn't over, she was deeply tormented. As she shared her story with me, I wondered what I could do for her? God has creative ideas. . . . I asked her to come outside with me. I took a large rock from the stone waterfall my husband had built. I handed it to her and said, "Let's go for a walk." Very soon she was huffing and puffing and told me she couldn't carry the rock any longer. (The longer we carry something the heavier it becomes.) My reply was, "You must carry it further." Minutes passed on our walk and she stopped and said, "I can't carry it anymore." I handed her a magic marker and said, "Name the rock." With tears, she wrote the name of the offender on the rock and we prayed for release and she threw the rock as hard as she could into the woods with the understanding she was giving it to God. Did this stop her pain? Momentarily.

The instruction going forward was *every time the anger arises*, tell God, I gave you the rock. Tell the devil, go home—go to hell—I gave God the rock, and tell yourself: "I gave the rock to God."

Months later I was speaking at a church and this lady came running toward me with a giant smile and her arms wide open. The plague had ended. . . .

To Spite or Not to Spite

Spite is the complete cut off point of love. Cancel culture is rooted in spite. When we are offended, we often use spite as the answer to offenses. There have been people in all of our lives that have done things that are truly awful and hurtful. The response comes as we begin *the inner vow.* Those vows build the great wall of offence. I know I have, and I know you have used inner vows to pick up spite stones to use as the rocks of revenge. Do you want to be the first one to throw a stone in any situation? Every spite holds a consequence, and those consequences leave us in a place of bitterness. It's like drinking poison and hoping the other person will die. After the cut off, we move on with a stubborn wall erected around our heart with signs on the wall saying—Keep Out! We think we are free. . . .

It's been said that there is no such thing as part freedom.

We need will power. Not our will, but *His* will. This cannot be manufactured by us; it is not humanly possible. It won't come from how good you and I are. It only comes through humility and submitting to God. Apart from Him, we can do nothing.

The real truth is that God loves that other person as much as He loves you and me. That is why He will use our situation to show His will through our willingness.

Broken Relationships

All you need for a dysfunctional family to exist is for that family to have more than one person in it. "If you cannot get rid of the family skeleton, you may as well make it dance." In the dance of life, it does take two to tango. It takes two to break a relationship. Broken relationships are like chasms and craters with a fault line running into the abyss. *Unforgiveness poisons the purity of purpose in life.*

My sister and I grew up very differently. We lived in

the same house with the same family but our ideas of what we loved were vastly different and as a result we lived in two different worlds. I was into horses and she was into fashion. We loved each other, but as many siblings do, we had a breach happen in our relationship. This disconnect lasted eight long years. These were years of torment. We both went on living our lives, tending to our own homes, families, and children, but deep inside there was always the hidden knowing that unforgiveness was ruling our hearts. That's what unforgiveness does, *it rules the heart.* Try as we might, we could not reconcile.

Rehearsing a hurt will cause the fault line of blame to widen. Every time you tell your story to someone or to yourself, the story becomes a chasm and chasms easily become craters. We end up wearing out a path in our minds from overthinking about an offense, and we slip into that path daily. If you have ever walked a trail over and over there is no more grass growing on it. It's just dirt. It's been walked over so much nothing can grow.

All it takes is a little bit of rain to change dirt into soil.

When we are hurt, most of us want to dump the truckload of boulders of pain we carry onto the other person. The way we deliver something is 90 percent of how people receive it. Now I know what I didn't know then: you have to build a bridge before you unload a truck, and bridges are not easy to build. In order to bridge with others, you have to meet them where they are at, not where you want them to be.

God uses all kinds of bridges to get our hearts across the bridge He builds. The bridge for my sister was a book by Ann Graham Lotz called *Wounded by God's People.* My bridge was formed after attending the funeral of a young woman, which highlighted to me the reality of how short life really is.

When it was all said and done, my sister and I met in a diner and within one minute, eight years of broken relationships melted the boulders. Our hearts met in the center of the bridge. I am so thankful and grateful because my sister is now my greatest friend.

If He can do it for me, He can do it for you.

Forgive 490 times. Seven times seventy according to Jesus. The great wall will come down.

Love is not easily angered and keeps no record of wrongs. Take a deep breath.

Money Can't Clean Your Love

Those who study trees know that trees with the strongest deepest roots have roots that are actually able to grow right through rocks. The root that is the largest is called the *taproot.* Interestingly, the wild fig tree in South Africa has roots that measure up to four hundred feet deep. The roots grow because they are looking for water and nutrients as well as providing a structure for the tree.

Just as the roots provide a foundation for the tree, the spiritual heart of man has a taproot that is deep-seated. This taproot is looking for nourishment to satisfy its heart's desire. Stability has nourishment as its key. The deep root in the heart of every person grows in one of two directions. The taproot in your heart will love God or love money, grow toward God or grow toward money. *The root of all evil is the love of money.* Money is a bad master if you become mastered by it. Unfortunately, when we are driven by the prostitution of money, the world suffers. When we trust in money more than trusting in God, we become a wild root wandering away; we stop looking for our true source. You can't serve to masters; you will love one and hate the other.

The shoots of these deep weeds toward money have grown and are alive today in every facet of life, especially so in sex trafficking, rape, and abortion where they grow in the soil of evil and bring disgrace to life and damage to the soul. There are few areas of life untouched by these weeds.

Love does not delight in evil. Take a deep breath.

Friends

The best friendships in life last the longest. The key is to *be*. Be the best friend to yourself and you will be that best friend to others. Friendships often come and go and superficial friendships don't last. All of us have imperfections. Loving unconditionally closes its eyes to imperfections. Maybe that's why dogs are said to be man's best friend.

Not everybody needs to know everything. Be careful who you tell your secrets to. Choose wisely. Our choices are the only real thing we own in this life. It's our choices that determine everything and we make thousands every day. Just like the five fingers on your hand, if you find your five trusted friends, you have struck gold. They will hold you in the palm of their hand, and catch your tears in a bottle. The truest friends won't stroke you; they'll push you forward and continually sharpen your sword with honest truth. The welcome mat of friendship lays down its life, allowing you to wipe your muddied feet that have stepped in manure on their clean mat, knowing your mess will turn out to be your message. The time spent in advice, laughter, tears, hopes, dreams, fears, and food is never wasted—it's cherished.

Love always protects. Take a deep breath.

Surrender Is the Flag Planted in Trust

"When it becomes more difficult to suffer than to change, that's when real change happens." *Please read that again slowly.*

Our healing is much more of a process than we realize. As a coach, one thing I can tell you is that people who are willing to go through the process end up with results. It takes digging deep. The instant fix is just a Band-Aid repair and your wound will fester again. Deep wounds seem bottomless and you have to be willing to dive in headfirst, then everything else follows. The road to surrender is long but if you're willing to take that road, healing is the destination point.

My son Daniel (DB), (Dben as we call him and my knight in shining armor as I call him), suffered with warts on his hands all of his middle and high school years. Not just one wart, but his hands were covered with atrocious, ugly, painful warts. During his adolescent years of playing basketball, noticing girls, and identity being shaped, you can imagine how insecure this made him feel, along with people staring and whispering. Those whispers became a source of chilling murmurs, and murmurs became the source of shame. DB is one of the greatest human beings I know. His quiet sadness and pain could not be hidden and my heart broke to watch him suffer. Worry is like a wart, it multiplies overnight.

We are a missions-minded family—collectively, among the four of us, we have been to over forty countries on mission trips. Daniel was getting ready to go on a mission trip to Swaziland, South Africa. Right before the trip we brought him to a top dermatological specialist who told us he had never seen a case of warts so severe. His recommendation was to soak Daniel's hands in Clorox, along with medication and burning therapy. He said it would take months to heal with no guarantee of any kind of results. We decided that after the trip we would start this regimen.

The week in Swaziland brought Daniel on a hike by himself to a place on a mountain and to a place deep in his own heart. He recalled being at the point of agony; his hands had been bleeding. The choice he made on that mountain was to trust the God who made the mountain. He gave his pain to God, truly surrendering it to Him. I can't tell you what that looked like because I wasn't there. Words on a page don't tend to do justice to the experience of the moment. But what I can tell you is that DB knew that surrender had taken place because of the unexplainable peace that followed.

When peace arrives in your circumstance, worry departs. DB never thought about his hands for the days following his mountaintop experience. Three days later, at a breakfast in the orphanage, someone asked him how his hands were. As he looked down at his hands, the warts were completely gone. I remember him getting off the plane running toward me and instead of hugging me, he held his hands up to my eyes. I tear up even as I write this now. We brought him back to that doctor, who was stunned—he only had one word for what he saw . . . "miracle." The long road is the cast-your-cares-to-Him road, the surrender-your-pain-to-Him road, the game-changer road, and it leads to miracle healing.

Love always trusts. Take a deep breath.

Train Tracks of Hope and Perseverance

It's not what side of the tracks you come from; it's staying on the tracks that moves you forward.

The train tracks of life are meant to take us to a destination. On track, we are on time, on target, and moving forward into a good future, purpose, and destiny. Just like a train that derails, when you experience disappointment, discouragement, or uncertainty you can be sent off the rails. One of the great causes of derailment is regret, and it defers our hope. It keeps us constantly stuck in the past. I know you wouldn't drive your car looking backward, so why approach your life that way?

Every time you look back your hope gets shelved; dust collects in your heart because you stop using your hope.

Yes, you have to *use* your hope. You may be one who says, "I don't have any hope." Here is a newsflash: hope is in you because God put it there and He polishes the dust off of our hearts through encouragement. Hope and encouragement are the rails of the train of life that will cause perseverance in us. They give us limitless possibilities to our God given potential. When we are off track it takes a pause in life to get back on the rails again. When we reach a point of knowing we need help, the pause happens. The pause may come in an unexpected circumstance. When it does, we are ready for HELP:

Hold—Everything—Loosely—Please. Let it go. Let it go. Let it go.

We don't know how to do that well. We want control. Controlling and micromanaging everything is fear based. Control wants power over something or someone. Control tries to play God. No matter what it looks like, God is still in control of the universe but He allows us to make own our choices.

If you want help, it will take "mailing" a letter. When you mail a paper letter, you let it go by dropping the envelope into a mailbox. You cannot reach back into the mailbox to get it out, as that would be illegal. It now belongs to the postmaster general and He is going to take it to where it is supposed to go.

When you let go of something to God, let it go with that understanding. It means it now belongs to Him. This is the caveat, either Jesus died or He didn't, either His blood was shed or it wasn't. Either He owns our pasts or He doesn't. Either you give Him control or you don't.

Which is it? Your life and freedom depend on your faith choice.

Love always hopes, loves always perseveres. Take a deep breath.

Unfailing Love

A few years ago, we were running a prayer tent at a festival on Cape Cod. People came into the tent all day wanting personal prayer. We had a team with us and we prayed for hundreds of people throughout the day. By 9:00 p.m. I told my husband, "I'm overdone, I can't pray for one more person, I'm tired, it's cold . . . can we please close?" Many were still in the tent, but thankfully Dan heard my heart and compassionately said, "Five more minutes." I sat down at the front of the tent, hoping and praying no one else would come in when I saw a beautiful woman heading straight for me. She sat down in the chair in front of me and boldly asked me, "How do I get saved?" This is not a usual question. I actually said to her, "Are you kidding?" She explained to me that she was from Colorado and was in Boston to visit her dying brother who had begged her to find God. He died shortly after her visit. Somehow, she ended up at this festival and saw our sign that said, 'Prayer Tent,' and she thought to herself, this must be the place to find God.

I asked her if she knew how to swim? She questionably looked at me and said, "Yes, I know how to swim." I continued, "Do you swim in the ocean?" Again, with a squinted, confused, questioning look, she said, "I have swum in the ocean before." I told her, "Picture yourself swimming in the ocean. A wave comes and pulls you out deeper. You begin to struggle more and another wave comes. Panic begins to set in as another wave now engulfs you and leaves you unable to catch your breath. Soon you are drowning, coughing, and choking, helpless—there is nothing that you can do to save yourself. You can't even yell for help. *Oh My God* is a fleeting thought and prayer— (Even any inside whisper of His name gets His attention).

The lifeguard sees you. He knows you're drowning and that you need help. *I HAVE TO SAVE THIS WOMAN.* He swims out to save you and rescues you back to shore. He breathes life back into you. When you wake up and look up, you see this man who saved you. You are so thankful, you are so grateful, you are so happy to be alive. You recognize and acknowledge—*He saved me.*

That night, Jesus saved that beautiful woman.
Love never fails. Take a deep breath

CHAPTER 9

EVERYTHING HAS BEEN DESIGNED FOR LOVE

Marriage Matters

MARRIAGE IS DEFINITELY A TWO-WAY STREET. I REMEMBER going to a marriage conference when I was first married to Dan. The speaker put two giant boxes up on the screen in front of us. One box was filled to capacity with exclamation points, zigzag lines, circles, and dashes signifying the brain of a woman. The other box had just one switch in the center of it signifying the brain of a man. The speaker said, "this is the difference between how a woman thinks and how a man thinks." . . . I never forgot that.

The affection of love is both verbal and physical. For some, to say "I love you" is a statement of commitment; for others it's a statement that they are craving temporary attention. The words of love are only words until there is action behind them. Love gives, and gives, and keeps giving. Love songs have been written for centuries, movies and plays are centered around love, all trying to describe the anointing of love.

The physical touch and intimacy of love are part of human desire. It is said that two people in love have the same heartbeat. When Dan and I met, we went on one date before he moved to Florida. We were thousands of miles away from each other but that couldn't stop our love. Wild horses could not keep Dan and me apart. We would find the hours and time to send love letters to one another. There were members of our family who didn't want our love to survive, but nothing can stop true love. We have thirty-eight years of devotion to one another. We found out quickly that in marriage love is a decision. Dan has always made me feel that my happiness is more important than his. We have had many bumps and bruises along the way, but true love can withstand the tide of fights. For love to go the distance it must let go of hurt, and hurdle disappointments. Love understands we may have failed, but we are not failures. Love matures like fine wine; it gets better with age. If I am honest, the cry of my heart is always "ask me what I feel, " and the cry of his is "more physical love." In coaching, I can tell you that resonates with a lot of couples. Both are made of intimacy—one emotional and one physical. *In-to-me-see* (intimacy) is to look beyond the flaws and see the depths of love inside. The key is to keep your eyes off the flaws. Love looks at what's right and not at what's wrong. All marriages connect so many people and the effects of love for good or bad change lives forever, especially in children.

Nature

I love everything to do with nature because nature reveals so much about love. There is a balance of relationships that exist in nature. There are odd couples, partnerships, and mutual protection found in the plant and animal kingdoms. There are the struggles of survival coupled with mysterious transformations of wildlife that leave room for us to learn.

Creation reveals the intricacy and captures the magnificence of its creator. Every detail is from the creative hand of God and holds absolute perfection and beauty for us to enjoy. The majesty of the universe should leave us in awestruck wonder, capturing our attention and helping us see life in its wholeness. The ability of our hearts to retain beauty comes from nature and is evidenced by our talent in any form of artistry.

Every plant and animal—from the tiniest ant to the largest whale—blends subtly and in harmony with life around it. It all works together. We see teamwork, patience, adaptability, wisdom, strength, respect, determination, cooperation, and so much more.

Gary Smalley once taught on personalities, likening them to animals. He used four types of animals—the Lion, the Beaver, the Otter, and the Golden Retriever. The lion is strong and courageous, the beaver is a builder and worker, the otter is fun loving and carefree, and the golden retriever is loyal and obedient. We all have a dominant personality, but to be well-rounded, flexible, and cooperative takes all of these qualities. Learning from nature has big benefits for flourishing love in our lives.

Time Is Expensive

Time is a teacher and a healer. There really is no time like the present, because it is a present. Don't forget who gave it to you. Use your time wisely; you can't be in two places at once, so wherever you are, be fully there. There is no waste of time in lessons learned. In life, there can be moments when you feel like you are out of time. **Don't wait.** "Say it in the living years." Giving time is one of the greatest ways to show love. Regrets in life often happen because we missed the time we could have spent with another person. That time will never be recovered.

My brother-in-law Johnny's kidneys failed and dialysis became a weekly regimen. He battled this difficulty courageously at every turn. His amazing, kind, loving wife and two exceptional boys honored him to the very end. The last few years of his life we spent almost every Sunday with Johnny and his family sharing a meal and time together. That quality time blew a hole in our differences. None of that mattered. What mattered was that we were all together. What mattered was that we could embrace the moments. What mattered was taking love to the limitations of life and living love without limits. What matters is that Johnny's place in heaven now is surrounded by God's glory. Time is valuable, spend it with love.

Giving and Receiving with Love

God's vineyards of the world are everywhere, waiting for those who would serve and give. Opportunities to love your neighbor as yourself are as close to home as next door and as far as the ends of the earth. The pure motive of love answers the call of needs. Motives are the drivers of the givers and takers of this world. Motives often have hidden agendas. Love doesn't enable, love provides. Love does not control, love trusts. Love does not manipulate, love serves. The test in the hardest conditions of humanity is dependent on the surety that love never fails. In sacrificial giving, you will always receive more than you give. When one is willing to say "send me, use me" sanctification of character, health of soul, and likeness to God shines. It may mean sacrifice, and it also may mean you will be part of a miracle.

Gratitude and Health in Love

Attitude and health are related. A tranquil mind is health to the body. When people are truly happy, they glow with radiant light. A merry heart does good like medicine. When your heart vibrates with joy and praise, the energizing power erupts like a geyser of love pouring from you. Pleasant words are like a honeycomb, sweet to the soul and health to the bones.

Gratitude is never empty to those who have been forgiven much. It's been my intention to love through these pages. It was not by chance, it was by choice. It's been a labor of love, for sure, and I've had to push and breathe with every step. The pressure only came from myself. During the writing, God kept me on the potter's wheel, so I could be redefined. Now that this book has been birthed, I am so grateful it produced something positive in me. I am positive *love never fails*. I have tried my best to write Life Words, planting the seeds of success of love in the soil of open hearts. To be able to represent some portion of

God's extravagant love to people is a privilege that I am so grateful and thankful for.

Whether you already know Him or are somewhere along the way, God is wildly in Love with you. His thoughts and plans for you are good. It is time to open your heart, open His word, and begin a new conversation with Him today.

His love is waiting to be experienced, and His gentle whispers are waiting to be heard. Take a moment even now to slow down, maybe even stop altogether and reach out to Him. His love is waiting to be discovered.

You will seek me and find me when you seek me with all your heart.

CHAPTER 10

THE EXPRESSIONS OF LOVE

Love Confronts

THERE ARE TWO SIDES TO EVERY STORY—BUT EVERY STORY has only one outcome. Jim Trick and I are friends, but love's confrontation has made us extraordinary friends.

Jim's side: "Over a decade ago, someone had the compassionate courage to confront me about the fact that I had become morbidly obese. She was direct, strong, clear, and kind. Her kindness wasn't soft though. It would have been so easy to say, 'who do you think you are?' or 'what about the things in your life?' Instead I decided to listen, open my heart, and receive what she had to say. I had a conversation about Don Miguel Ruiz's book, *The Four Agreements*. One of his agreements is not to take anything personally. 'Take' is an interesting word. Taking something personally is the path to being offended, hurt, or upset. Ruiz famously said 'the whole world can gossip about you, and if you don't take it personally you are immune.' I had a choice to be offended or not to be offended. I had the choice to be crushed or not crushed. I had the choice to be hurt or not hurt. I also had the choice that I didn't consider until that morning—and here it is: I had the choice to apply her words personally without taking them personally. Now, still over two hundred pounds lighter, that choice has made all the difference. Thank you, Gina Blaze, for your courage and care. All these years later I'm still deeply in your debt."

My side: Jim is a good friend even though I only see him once a year. What brings us together is an annual music festival in New Hampshire. Jim is a singer/song-writer and has the gift of humor. People at the festival flock to Jim's stage to experience his musical talent and to be refreshed by joy and laughter. My husband and I have run the prayer tent at that festival for the last twenty-two years. One evening as I watched Jim walking toward me at our tent, I thought to myself, "He's going to die." Jim sat down in front of me with a big smile, and said "give it to me, I'm ready for some love." That was the door. I love this man enough to speak the truth. I know he didn't expect what I was about to say and honestly, I don't think I did either. I looked at Jim directly and told him it was time to do something about his weight. Confrontation gets in the way of concealments. We talked about what was holding him back from facing this head on. I prayed for Jim. As uncomfortable as it is, confronting someone you love with love always sparks hope. Jim would send updates throughout his weight loss journey and his trans-parency and victory has given so many people the spark of hope for themselves toward freedom.

Love Sees Your Star

The New England Prayer Center has hosted many speakers

from around the world. When we invite a speaker, we don't send people to hotels. We have a guestroom in our home and believe in breaking bread and building relationship with every person. Sometimes speakers come here to just take a break, not to do ministry. We received a call from a pastor from across the country who asked if he could come to take a rest, regroup, and get quiet for a little while. It was an honor and a blessing to have him choose this place to come when he could have gone anywhere. The day he arrived we shared a meal and he shared a heartbreak. The situation had brought shame and discouragement to him. Often people who are in the limelight cannot share trials and troubles because of judgment and need a place to just be and heal. We told him, "as long as you're here, our house is yours." Whatever his need was, we would pray for him.

Knowing he was hurting about his very personal situation we thought about doing something that would bring encouragement to him. One evening we asked him to come and sit in front of the picture window overlooking a field from our dining room. We had closed the curtain so he could not see out the window. We told him that God wanted him to know how He saw him, in spite of the way he saw himself. As the curtains opened in the darkness, what he saw was a giant star on the field with his own name in bright lights. It brought tears and truth.

We reminded him that God told Abraham to look up at the sky and count the stars: *every one of them is your offspring.* We reminded him, *"Those who are wise will shine like the brightness of the heavens and those who lead many* to righteousness, *like the stars for ever and ever"* and we reminded him: *"Do everything without grumbling or arguing, so that you may become blameless and pure, children of God without fault in a warped and crooked generation. Then you will shine among them like stars in the sky."*

You, my dear reader, are a shining star.

Love's Acceptance and Grace

My daughter Lindsay's story in her own words . . .

My favorite thought about grace is the idea that sparks will fly when grace collides with a life. Grace can be defined by one moment in time. My day of grace was the day I told my parents my story and it was everything they hoped they would never hear. At the end of it all, my Dad said to me, "In your life, every accomplishment, all you've done and the places you've been, I have never been prouder of you than this moment." And I thought, what father hears about a wayward daughter and is proud of her? Had I ever experienced such a thing as this before . . . this thing called grace?

Grace hears and sees and knows the worst of who we are but stares straight at the best of who we are. Grace sees the Creator in the created, and in that place, that's where sparks fly because something about grace changes everything. It takes the state of our mind and our heart and connects it to the truth of our soul. Do you want to know about your soul, then set your eyes to the Heavens, because that is where your soul comes from. When the sky displays colors that you can't even name, when it opens up and pours down rain and cracks thunder and blazes lightning, when the stars come out and you feel the depth of your humble place, you know very well your soul comes from the same One that would dare to create such things in the sky.

He decided to make you—that's grace. That's grace.

So, give grace and live grace and receive grace and watch those sparks fly, because Heaven has collided with earth in you. Let that seed of grace grow, for you are good soil.

Let the sparks of grace fly.

The Love Song of Deliverance Over Tragedy

On December 14, 2012 the Sandy Hook Elementary school in Newtown, Connecticut became the focus of the whole world. We all watched in complete shock and horror what was unfolding on our television. We live twenty-five minutes away from that school and Dan and I were trying to decide what we should do in response to this horrific tragedy. We called our friend in Colorado, Bruce Porter, who was a first responder at the Columbine shooting years before. Bruce addressed the nation on CNN when that tragedy happened. He told us to "Get in your car and go."

We arrived in Sandy Hook at 4:00 p.m. on the day of the shooting. At the police checkpoint, Dan handed a policeman our card stating that we were from the New England Prayer Center and we were waved through. It was like a war zone; there was complete chaos. As we were passing people on the street, we could see and feel the numbness on people's faces throughout the town—it seemed like nobody knew which way to go. We ended up in a church in the center of town where several of the families who had lost children attended. Sometimes the only thing you can do in a time of crisis is to hug and cry with people. That's exactly what we did for hours that night.

The next morning, as I sat in my kitchen sharing the sadness along with the rest of the country, I began to pray. The loss and devastation of this unimaginable tragedy had left me speechless. In my spirit I heard the Lord say, "Use my Words." I didn't know exactly what that meant until later.

A few weeks before this tragedy, I had been in a thrift store. I had called my husband from the store to ask if he wanted me to purchase a box that had about one hundred sets of brand-new white Christmas lights in it. For ten dollars, this was a find. Meanwhile my husband had brought three large pieces of plywood into our garage, each as big as a Volkswagen not knowing what he would use them for, but Dan always creates a magical surprise every Christmas.

As I was contemplating "Use my Words," Dan walked into the kitchen, and I told him what I had heard God speak in my spirit. He looked at me pondering, but never told me what he was about to do. All day Dan was in our garage, creating. Dan painted the three pieces of plywood black, and used the white Christmas lights to spell out three words: Faith, Hope, and Love on each piece of plywood. Early that evening, a team of men assembled at our home to help with the plan and we all headed back to Newtown. Overnight, the town of Sandy Hook had been taken over by newscasters from around the world. People were coming from all over the country to support families, and the memorial of love had begun to sprout and grow on the main street with teddy bears, flowers, signs, and all kinds of love tokens.

We parked at the church where we had been the night before and were told we could set up the "three words" on the side of the church property. Immediately, I knew it was not the spot, but we didn't want to be disagreeable, and we were there to honor, not impose. I prayed again and again I heard in my spirit, "Go to the high point." I told Dan I was going to take a walk while they assembled the signs. I went down the street to the very center of town where the growing memorial was. Directly across the street from it was a "high point" where an old Victorian building/house had been converted to offices and apartments.

I walked up the lawn to the front door and knocked. It was dark inside and I knew no one was there. I turned the front door handle and to my surprise the door was open. (I believe when a door opens you go through it.) I began to call out, "Is anybody here, hello, is anybody here?" I looked up the stairway and saw a dim light. Following the light, I went and knocked on the door at the top of the stairway. A woman answered and I explained why I was there. She immediately told me to bring the signs. I ran back to the church and the signs had been put up where we were instructed to put them, but the power to light them *would not work*. Three different attempts were made to try to light the signs but there was no electrical power. I told my husband that God showed me the spot for the signs and that we were clear to put them in front of the building at the high point of town. The team of men walked the signs down the street to the high point (across from the growing memorial that was forming), and they were erected with the help of the woman living in the building. She graciously supplied us with extra electric extension cords, coffee, and kindness. The memorial quickly became the focal point where most reporters nationally and internationally were reporting from, and now the words *Faith*, *Hope*, and *Love* were brightly displayed in the background of these newscasts. They are God's three words. They became the mantra for Newtown's tragedy—not because we did it, but because God did it. Wristbands were made with those words and newscasters used those words. People held tight to those three words . . . and hope and healing began.

About ten days later, right before Christmas, we were again praying for the families who had lost their precious children when we heard God say, "Sing over the town." It was the Friday evening before Christmas. We assembled a small team of musicians (a keyboardist, guitar player, and two singers) and we went to the porch of the high point building and began to sing softly over the town. The problem was, there were three generators that had been set up to shine bright lights on the memorial. They were vibrating with a constant monotone loud sound in the street right in front of us. There was a state trooper who was watching what we were doing. I looked at him and he looked back at me. He nodded at me, and he walked over to each generator and one-by-one he shut them off.

Our team began to sing softly, sweetly, and gently. A very supernatural happening occurred. As we began to sing

"Silent Night" people began to gather on the lawn to join us. People came out of bars and restaurants, off the streets, and even some of the newscasters who were still reporting joined in. There was a spontaneous choir assembled of dozens and dozens of people singing in harmony "silent night" over the town of Sandy Hook. Scripture says there is a song of deliverance and surely, on this holy night, that was the one for Sandy Hook. Later one of the newscasters (one who we all recognize) came up to me with tears in his eyes. He said he hadn't been to church since he was a little boy but church came to him that night. Tragedies are no small thing in life. God can make beauty out of ashes.

CHAPTER 11

THE POWER OF LOVE

People who only believe what they can see, will never believe what they can't see.

AS A COACH, I HAVE ENCOUNTERED MANY PEOPLE WHO only believe what they can see with their physical eyes. But it is what you don't see with your eyes that provides you with revelation power. Revelation is the true agent of change. Logic adds up, but revelation *powers up*. The power of love never runs out. It's like an unstoppable unending waterfall. God pours out His Spirit on people. He doesn't measure, He pours. Like golden raindrops, His love will water a life to give a heart of pure gold. The most prized and cherished position we all have is to use the platform that has been given to us to exhibit the greatest power within us. Whether you are a mother, friend, creator, journalist, CEO, lawyer, doctor, or anything else, you are full of the power of love.

The Power of Love in Unity

Unity is not doing the same thing; unity is having the *same goal*. In such a disconnected world when unity seems elusive, the universal language of music transcends differences and unifies diverse people to the heart of the song. Concerts bring people together who sing in unified harmony that otherwise might never mingle.

The universal language of your smile is your first power source. It has no language, race, social, or economic barrier. It unifies the hearts of people. Interesting that we all have to wear masks at this time in history. Also interesting, one of the meanings of the Hebrew name for God, Yahweh—means to breathe. There is no exclusiveness to smile or to breathe, they are totally universal to every human being. A deep breath and a smile changes everything.

Jesus prayed for unity:

Not for these only do I pray, but for those also who will believe in me through their word, that they may all be one; even as you, Father, are in me, and I in you, that they also may be one in us; that the world may believe that you sent me. The glory which you have given me, I have given to them; that they may be one, even as we are one; I in them, and you in me, that they may be perfected into one; that the world may know that you sent me and loved them, even as you loved me.

The Power of Love in Tears

To tap a tree, you must drill a hole and wound the tree at the right time and the right season. When tapped, a tree produces a defensive chemical that is antifungal and antibacterial to protect itself. Interestingly, our tears produce an antifungal, antibacterial chemical to rid the body of toxins. The tree never volunteered to be tapped, and tears are involuntary bodily functions. There is strength in tears. Most of us are told from an early age to "stop crying," but the reality is that tears enable us to get in touch with our deepest feelings and to get in touch with God.

In the earliest years of humanity, the regard for "the gift of tears" was likened to the breaking of waters of the womb before the birth of a child, making the connection between pain and joy. There are 697 references to tears in the Bible and there are six types of tears: tears of sorrow, tears of joy, tears of compassion, tears of desperation, tears of travail, and tears of repentance. I gave my husband a bumper sticker that said *Real Men Cry*. I was sad when it came time to sell that truck because of that sticker. The next time you feel like crying, don't suppress your tears because tears are a power source; they are liquid prayer.

The Power of Love in Honesty

Love is honest.

Honesty gives positive virtuous attributes such as integrity, truthfulness, and straightforwardness along with the absence of lying. Honesty has become abnormal in the new normal.

Years ago, one of my dearest friend's son was getting married. My good friend was helping to plan the wedding and her desire was to bless her son and new daughter-in-law's marriage in every way that she could. My friend is a very quiet giant and she carries herself in a shy manner. Loving people is her ultimate goal. She shared with me that she had purchased her dress from an exclusive shop in Mount Kisco, New York. She asked me if I would go to the fitting with her and see the dress. I was happy to accommodate and be privy and part of her wardrobe choice. We arrived at this posh bridal shop where she was well attended by the employees, escorting her to the fitting room to try on the dress. She had already purchased the dress, which was very expensive, and first alterations had already been done. While she was in the fitting room, I was watching as another woman had come out to the mirror where I was sitting. I admired her elegant, beautiful gown. We began to chat and she shared with me that this was her second marriage and the dress she had chosen was not a formal wedding dress. It was a beautiful cream-colored silhouette dress and she looked absolutely elegant in it.

Minutes later, my friend stepped out of the fitting room, and in my heart, I gasped at what I saw. The dress she had chosen did not flatter her in any way, shape, or form. The color was green as grass and in all honesty, I thought, "How did this happen?" The women who were working in the shop were giving her accolades about how great the dress looked on her. My thoughts were the complete opposite. My friend asked "What do you think?"

This was a crossroads moment. Do I tell the truth or do I go along with popular opinion and save offending her? Moments like this happen to all of us every day in life—truth or consequences.

I asked if I could have a few moments with my friend alone away from the employees of the shop. I looked her square in the eye and asked, "Do you like it?" The look on her face told me everything. "It's already been paid for and altered," she said, "and the wedding is just weeks away." I asked if she would try on another dress—the cream-colored silhouette dress that the woman who was getting married had on—which was also altered and purchased. After talking to the dear lady who was getting married, she agreed to let my friend try it on. Needless to say, the employees were not happy. This was not part of their policy.

My friend emerged from the dressing room with the cream-colored dress on and she looked magnificent in it. The look on her face told me everything.

I am a bold person and asked to see the owner of the shop. I explained to him what he already knew. How important a wedding day is and how important it is for the mother of the groom to be in an amazing dress. I told him that I didn't know why his employees would guide my friend to the green grass dress. Reputation means a lot in life and after our conversation, the owner felt obliged to work this matter out. Honesty won. The owner agreed to exchange the green grass dress for the beautiful cream-color dress for my friend. The woman agreed to allow my friend to have the dress because they could order her another one, as her wedding was months away (enough time for her to get a new one made). As we drove away from the shop, we laughed with joy over the miracle of the dresses. My friend wore that beautiful new cream dress proudly on her son's wedding day and she looked exquisite and confident. Honesty tells the truth; God wants honesty in love and uses it as the best policy.

The Power of Love in Creativity

Love Is Creative.

Many years ago, during Christmas season, when our kids were eleven and six years old, we began asking them what they wanted for Christmas. Bedtime was filled with stories, laughter, tickling, and prayer. Weeks before Christmas that year, our son would hold his hands in prayer, close his eyes, and ask God for snow on Christmas. Every night his prayer was the same. "Jesus, please let it snow for Christmas." We encouraged him that Jesus heard his prayer and would give him snow. The problem was the temperature that year was unusually warm. The week before Christmas the weather forecast was undesirable for snow—in fact, it was in the fifties and there was no snow coming. I told my husband to stop encouraging Daniel because I didn't want him to be disappointed. But my husband would keep assuring Daniel that God heard his prayer for snow on Christmas. The day before Christmas the forecast hadn't changed—there would be no white Christmas. I was annoyed with my husband because he told Daniel he would be sledding on Christmas Day. What I didn't know was that a plan of hope and future was thought of. My husband got up during the night on Christmas Eve and went with our friend Brian to the local ice rink. They shoveled the leftover ice that was piled up outside from the Zamboni into a pickup truck, packing it full to overflowing with the snow. There was enough snow to make our yard look like a winter wonderland and enough for a sled to run down the hill. My husband even arranged flags and a new sled ready to go. Christmas morning was filled with magic and our kids screamed with glee. Love is creative and accomplishes answers to prayer.

The Power of Love in Preparedness and Favor

Preparedness is to be ready to hurdle life's obstacles. Wholeness is to be restored mentally, spiritually, and physically. When we venture toward wholeness, we become more prepared. Many people wait until the last minute to get prepared, it's better to be ready in season and out. Noah built the ark before it rained one drop.

When you are prepared you can enjoy life more. Your stress level will go way down and your security and confidence level will go way up. You will be motivated and very intentional. You will gain respect in relationships, and have the ability to contribute in helping others. The multiplication of your wisdom will succeed. Being prepared accomplishes success. Success is something that you love so much that you're willing to do it for free but you're so good at it, people are willing to pay you for it. Success is who you are when God is with you. That's favor.

There is a reason for favor on your life; it is not to make you live more comfortably. Favor is given so that everyone around you thrives. Your influence, success, and accomplishments will attract the right and wrong people. Set your boundaries well.

While on my first mission trip to Africa, all my senses were on high alert. Everything was different and the unknown carries a healthy fear. We traveled three hours one way every day from Kenya to get to the mission location in Nakuru. Armed guards would enter our bus, there were no bathrooms except for a hole in the ground, there were flies on food, drought, children with AIDS, sickness, poverty, and dust storms. It seemed like we were as far out as you could be from civilization, yet hundreds of Masai people would walk miles and hours to get to where we were. They are a dancing people—colorful, joyous and resilient. I remember standing on a rickety chair speaking to hundreds of beautiful African women about God's healing mercies. When I stepped off the chair, I was shocked to be ambushed by all of these women who were desperate to touch me.

Later in the week, a surprise came as a motorcade of vehicles showed up in the desert where we were. The vice president of Kenya came to the place of this mission to dedicate a well that was being dug for water in this dry and thirsty land. A makeshift structure was erected to shade the dignitaries as drums were beating and people danced for him.

My friend, Pastor Mike Brawan from Kenya, pulled me aside and declared, "Gina you must come and give the Vice President a word." As he was saying this, he was already pulling me toward him. I was not prepared for this and tried to pull away. Mike does not take "no" for an answer. Before I blinked three times, I was standing in front of the vice president of Kenya. Yes, I closed my eyes and prayed and yes, I did give him a word. There was pressure in the moment. Pressure is greatest when there is the most to lose or the most to gain.

Favor is a blessing we all have, and becoming uniquely gifted in your work brings that blessing front and center. It will bring promotion and you will stand before kings. You are uniquely and wonderfully made and the favor of the Lord is upon you and surrounds you like shield.

The Power of Love in Memories

The memories we all carry of lost love ones are the points of reference on life's journey. Pain is very individual to each of us and no one can fully understand another person's pain. Memories connect us heart to heart. As I write this, it is September 11, 2020. Nineteen years ago today was one of the saddest days in America's history. America grew in love through empathy, sympathy, and tragedy. As every year passes, on the anniversary of 9/11 we commemorate and remember the courageous heroes and the lives lost that infamous day. The tributes reawaken pain but also bring love closer to home. We watch and listen to life stories, moments of silence, and names read one by one bringing celebration of life from death. God is always calling us to remember.

CHAPTER 12

THE PLANS OF LOVE

Help Is on the Way

MANY YEARS AGO, MY HUSBAND AND I ATTENDED A WEEK-
end conference. It was held at a beautiful retreat center
overlooking fields and mountains. In one of the last sessions the speaker gave us all an exercise. We were each
given a helium balloon and a magic marker. We were
instructed to take our balloon and write the names of
everyone that we needed to forgive. We all went off to a
quiet place to mark our balloons. Most people went outside, but I decided to stay inside and began to identify
offenses and hurts from people in my life that I hadn't
dealt with. My balloon began to fill with names and soon
the entire surface was covered and my own name appeared
last and biggest on the top of the balloon. Upon comple-
tion we were told to go out to the field and release our
balloon and watch it rise to the sky until we couldn't see
it anymore.

When I finished, instead of going out in the middle
of the field to release my balloon, I went to the balcony
of the beautiful conference center and prayed my prayer
of release to let go of years of hidden hurts and offenses
from people that I held captive in my heart. With a deep
breath and a deep wish, I let go of the string and released

my balloon to heaven, but an odd thing happened. My balloon suspended in front of me almost like it was staring at me, saying, "Are you sure?" I watched as a small breeze took the balloon as it floated slowly to the right of me. Suddenly, another wind came and carried my balloon past me again, as I watched it float toward the only tree in the field. I felt my heart sink as I saw my balloon head toward the tree. The branch reaching out from that tree grabbed my balloon. The tree had now captured it. "No, this can't be happening!" I ran out down to the tree totally dismayed that the balloon that held my healing was now held prisoner by the tree. I stared up at my red balloon like Charlie Brown, stuck in limbo and despair. All of the people who had just released their balloons were walking up from the field and saw my dilemma and they were quick to make a plan and suggestions on how to help me.

Within seconds one man was on top of another man's shoulders. Another man began to climb the tree, and still another got a large stick to try to reach the balloon. Minutes passed and soon the balloon was handed back to me. With a sigh of relief, I walked to the field and released my balloon to heaven. As I was walking back up, I heard the applause; it felt like all of heaven was clapping for me. The whisper in my spirit said this, *"when you are stuck in life, you need help from others. You can't do it alone."*

Love Shows Up

One of the hardest times of my life was going to see my brother who I hadn't seen in a few years. His life is ravaged by schizophrenia. He's one of the many "invisible people" on the earth today. I talked to my friend about my plans and how anxious and fearful I truly felt. I knew she would pray. My brother's illness leaves him tormented and delusional and has carried many painful memories for my entire family. I de-boarded the plane in Fort Lauderdale, not knowing my friend was de-boarding her plane from Sioux Falls, South Dakota to meet me in Florida. As I was walking through the airport, I was shocked to see my friend standing there. Judy Shaw showed up. That's what friends do; they just show up. She announced, "Let's go do this, together." Together we are better. Two is better than one. My comfort level went from fear to faith because she showed up.

The time spent with my brother brought solace to my heart. It was not easy, but Judy's presence made it easier.

When people we love are out of control and need help so desperately, doing what is the hardest is usually the catalyst for change.

Love Teaches

When God turns the page, He is writing a new chapter. Nothing will be as it was before. When the student is ready the teacher appears. It's been said that the shame of life would be leaving this earth without doing what you are born to do. Your career is what you're paid for, your calling is what you're made for.

Throughout life we meet all kinds of people. People are put in our path to teach us something. Madeline Balletta was put in my life to teach me about love. Madeline was made for love. She is my miracle friend and our hearts are supernaturally connected forever. We have years of milestones and memories.

Madeline has accomplished many things in her life. She ran a multimillion-dollar company, she has graced the cover of magazines, she has been hosted on national radio and television and been with headline celebrities. Yet, Madeline's devotion to Jesus has been left unscathed by all of that. She does not live her life privileged. She lives everyday with one determination; how can she love people more.

Every day of her life Madeline battles for her health. She was born without a particular group of antibodies imperative for the immune system. Many times, her life has been in the balance. She has been given many death diagnoses and has endured pain courageously. I have watched in awe as she fights for her health God's way. Everything Madeline does is filtered through the lens of His word and God has sustained her over and over. In the exploration to find answers to her health problems, I was blessed to accompany Madeline to Germany to a wellness center. People come to this place from all over the world, speaking different languages but all having the common goal of wellness.

During the two weeks I spent in Germany at this wellness center, the staff, the other guests, and others from the community all had the same reaction to Madeline: They felt loved. When you encounter Madeline, she doesn't just look at you, she looks inside of you, at your soul. Her love has changed countless lives for the better. I have been the recipient of her clean love and I am eternally grateful.

CHAPTER 13

THE HISTORY MAKERS: THOUGHTS ON LOVE

The Influencers

THE INFLUENCERS IN THE FACETS OF RELIGION, FAMILY, education, government, media, entertainment & arts, and business can change a nation. Throughout history the leaders in these mountains of influence have shaped who we are in many ways and the way we understand love. God gave us the understanding of the fact that there is a right way and a wrong way to approach Him. Some of the following statements are partial truths. They are only applicable in our relationship to God when they are included as part of God's bigger story. His love is in every facet of our multi-faceted life. The expression of God's love in these seven mountains of influence is to prepare us for success in life.

Billy Graham on Religion

"'God is love' means that He tries constantly to block your route to destruction."

Winston S. Churchill on Family

"There is no doubt that it is around family and the home that all the greatest virtues, the most dominating virtues of human society, are created, strengthened and maintained."

Martin Luther King Jr. on Education

"The function of education is to teach one to think intensively and to think critically. Intelligence plus character—that is the goal of true education."

Abraham Lincoln on Government

"Government of the people, by the people, for the people, shall not perish from the Earth."

George Orwell on Media

"The people will believe what media tells them to believe."

Walt Disney on Entertainment

"I would rather entertain and hope that people learned something than educate people and hope that they were entertained."

Thomas Edison on Business

"Many of life's failures are people who did not realize how close they were to success when they gave up."

The following are four examples of well know history makers who pointed to God in their own way. In their search these men found something bigger than what they could offer, they found something outside themselves that pointed to God.

Albert Einstein was the world's most famous genius.

"There are only two ways to live your life. One is though nothing is a miracle. The other is though everything is a miracle."

Gandhi is best remembered for his compassion, vision, tolerance, and patience.

"My imperfections and failures are as much a blessing from God as my success and my talents and I lay them both at his feet."

Sir Isaac Newton was recognized as the most influential scientist of all time. He gave us the understanding of gravity and the three basic laws of motion.

"All of my discoveries have been made in an answer to prayer."

"I believe the more I study science the more I believe in God."

Confucius was an influential Chinese philosopher, teacher, and political figure.

"Attack the evil that is within yourself rather than attacking the evil that is in others."

"Heaven means to be one with God."

All of these men were searching for truth. Jesus said truth is not an idea it's a person. "I am the way the truth and the life." Love is not transactional. Love is relational. Jesus taught love by example because He is the example.

Jesus. He was and is the most powerful, controversial person who ever lived on this planet. He was recognized as a prophet, a Jewish teacher, but not always believed to be the Son of God. Jesus's love through His compassion for people was limitless. Blind eyes were opened and the sick made well. People who suffered by demons were set free, and social injustices were made right through His magnificent love. His value for children, the poor, and women, which was culturally unaccepted in His time, was evident through respect and honor. Jesus lived out love because He is love.

"As I have loved you, so you must love one another."

"But I tell you, love your enemies and pray for those who persecute you, that you may be children of your Father in heaven."

"Love the Lord your God with all your heart and with all your soul and with all your strength and with all your mind; and, 'Love your neighbor as yourself.'"

"Greater love has no one than this: to lay down one's life for one's friends."

CHAPTER 14

THE PRAYERS OF 1000 GENERATIONS

PRAYER IS COMMUNICATION WITH GOD FOR THE INTERvention in humanity's affairs.

Right now, on the earth, God is building His prayer house. For the last thirty years my husband and I have been directors of the New England Prayer Center (NEPC). We have seen countless miracles accomplished through prayer. For many years we have been contending for the property where we operate the NEPC. We want to acquire the thirty acres to become a complete hope and healing center for all people—a center for the mind, the body, and the spirit. It has been a battle with a very long story that has had many twists and turns.

The NEPC has received a consistent word that "what happens on this land will affect the entire nation." We have stood on that word all these years. This land is set apart. It is divinely shaped, resembling the very borders of Israel's Holy Land. It has a heritage of faith in its foundation. We believe God wants to use this land for His purposes. A center of freedom. Prayer has been the sustaining factor of this incredible place. In your faith fight, determination is the champion. You can't win what you don't love. We love this land and even though it's taking a long time, we are not backing down or quitting.

Throughout history the benefits of a praying people cause us to remember and give thanks for His mercy and love to all generations. The overdue season of the church to invest in the most precious commodity of prayer is now. It's not time to be quiet. The thing the world needs most is prayer and prayer must become the language of the future. A disinterest in prayer exists because people became more interested and concerned about building their own houses than God's. Discouragement became a mindset, causing dissatisfaction from people who wanted immediate reversal to years and years of systemic problems. Adversity has come, but God has always used adversity to change the difficulty of life into accomplishment and success.

Billions and billions of prayers through all generations have all been heard by God. One of the Hebrew names of God is Jehovah Shama—*the God who is already there*. He's already in our future. All of God's plans for our great future are bound up in prayer. There is and always will be a remnant of people who will continue to PUSH—Pray-Until-Something-Happens, in prayer. The people who love God and His purposes don't stop praying till He says so. Ready or not, they are living in a revival state of mind, and fires of prayer will burn bright. The reset humans are searching for will only happen through prayer. Prayer opens the way and allows God's love to shine. Words are the voice of the heart, and effectual fervent prayer declares God's words.

The place of prayer is the most confident place we can go because He is faithful and keeps His covenant of Love to a thousand generations. Prayer is what the world needs now.

To the Church:

Though many people act this way, we do not live in a holy country club. In Jeremiah Johnson's book, *Judgment on the House of God: Cleansing and Glory Are Coming*, he says, "If the church is going to be visited by the angel of glory, she must first receive the angel of cleansing." Proverbs 31 was written by a man named King Lemuel, whose name means consecrated to God/holy. His mother dedicated him to God. The pen is his but the words are hers. "Don't be a drunk, keep yourself pure. Know right from wrong. Speak out for justice for the people who have no voice and stand up for the poor" (paraphrased). Proverbs 31 gives us a picture of the Bride of Destiny, the Church. She is not a superhero; she is a bride. When the "cleansing" is finished, the question of "will you marry me" will be answered by a readied bride. This proverb tells us the result of a pure and spotless bride:

> "She is uniquely qualified in prayer, rivers flow from her. She is not spiteful or resentful. She is unoffendable. She is resourceful and frugal. She is generous and willing to work. She is an entrepreneur. She is prepared; already stored up for next season. With wisdom and discernment, she thinks a thing through. She knows how to manage money; she lives in an overflow and has extra. She is not afraid, a positive thinker and runs to help the needy. She spiritually works out, is dressed in color, and life is thriving around her. She has goals and new goals. She is kind

and Her wisdom won't allow laziness, her family has respect and blesses her. She lives in the fear of the Lord and is optimistic about the future. Her husband trusts her. She is Happy, Holy, Healthy, and at Peace."

—*Gina Blaze*

CHAPTER 15

AMERICA

AMERICA IS A GREAT NATION. AS A COUNTRY, AMERICA IS beautiful and we all hold a great privilege to live in the land of the free and the home of the brave. We are an amazing people filled with resilience, diversity, and strength. God truly has given Americans an unstoppable spirit. The single most important element in America is the belief that all men were created equal. Built into America's founding is the pathway to freedom. The founding principles of America are honorable and worth remembering. Honor is not lost but it definitely needs to be found again. Plain and simple, honor values others. The Declaration of Independence signing included the American founding fathers agreeing with each other's lives, fortunes, and sacred honor. I have researched honor and there has been a case made that honor comes in two types: horizontal and vertical. Horizontal honor is mutual respect, and respect is a two-way street. The code of honor in mutual respect has standards, which must be reached. When people stop caring, honor loses its power. Horizontal honor gets the respect of your peers and either you have it or you don't.

Vertical honor it's not mutual respect, but it gives honor to those who serve the community and society—people who are authority figures in every sphere of influence—family, religion, business, politics, education, media, and the arts. The disregard of honor in America has affected every individual and every institution. Perversion is a curse that reverses the direction of something. The perversion of love has taken America in the wrong direction. The restitution of God is to return something to better than its original state.

America's answer is not political. It's not a Democrat or Republican issue. It's a God issue. The simplest, cleanest most natural understanding of life is to *love God with all your heart, soul, mind, and strength and to love your neighbor as yourself.* Love is an action word. There is an old Indian saying that says, "Before you judge, walk a mile in another man's shoes." This is to understand someone's experiences, challenges, and thought processes and to feel what another person is experiencing from their point of reference.

Returning to honor is the great challenge. My personal belief is that it will take great expectation. Expectation is the birthplace of miracles. Real love has great expectations.

Martin Luther King Jr. spoke these famous words from what he called hallowed ground and honored all lives because everyone matters:

I Have A Dream (in part)

I have a dream that one day every valley shall be exalted, every hill and mountain shall be made low, the rough places will be made plain, and the crooked places will be made straight and the glory of the Lord shall be revealed and all flesh shall see it together.

This is our hope. This is the faith that I go back to the South with. With this faith, we will be able to hew out of the mountain of despair a stone of hope. With this faith we will be able to transform the jangling discords of our nation into a beautiful symphony of brotherhood.

With this faith we will be able to work together, to pray together, to struggle together, to go to jail together to stand up for freedom together, knowing that we will be free one day.

This will be the day, this will be the day when all of God's children will be able to sing with new meaning: My country, 'tis of thee, sweet land of liberty, of thee I sing. Land where my fathers died, land of the pilgrim's pride, from every mountainside, let freedom ring! And if America is to be a great nation, this must become true. So let freedom ring from the prodigious hilltops of New Hampshire. Let freedom ring from the mighty mountains of New York. Let freedom ring from the heightening Alleghenies of Pennsylvania. Let freedom ring from the snow-capped Rockies of Colorado.

Let freedom ring from the curvaceous slopes of California. But not only that: Let freedom ring from Stone Mountain of Georgia. Let freedom ring from Lookout Mountain of Tennessee. Let freedom ring from every hill and molehill of Mississippi. From every mountainside, let freedom ring.

And when this happens, and when we allow

freedom to ring, when we let it ring from every village and every hamlet, from every state and every city, we will be able to speed up that day when all of God's children, black men, and white men, Jews and Gentiles, Protestants and Catholics, will be able to join hands and sing in the words of the old Negro spiritual: "Free at last! Free at last! Thank God Almighty, we are free at last!"

CHAPTER 16

THE DESTINATION OF LOVE: DO IT ANYWAY

THE MASTER PLAN OF LOVE WILL ACCEPT NOTHING LESS than the truest and purest heart. The immeasurable investment of worth in each of us from God is displayed in our intelligence, value, hope, honor, and love and should always carry the high mark of *very good*. Another day is given for a higher perspective. We own our every choice, especially the choice to be washed in God's love. To conquer with love takes a tremendous dependence on God. That extraordinary truth causes the impossible to become nothing, and gives everything unlimited possibilities. Clean Love's destination is to release love without limits. If you are willing, He is able. All of creation is waiting. Mother Theresa had a key. . . .

Do It Anyway

People are often unreasonable, illogical,
and self-centered.
Forgive them anyway.
If you are kind, people may accuse you of selfish,
ulterior motives.
Be kind anyway.
If you are successful, you will win some unfaithful
friends and some genuine enemies.
Succeed anyway.
If you are honest and sincere people may deceive you.
Be honest and sincere anyway.
What you spend years creating, others could destroy
overnight.
Create anyway.
If you find serenity and happiness, some may
be jealous.
Be happy anyway.
The good you do today, will often be forgotten.
Do good anyway.
Give the best you have, and it will never be enough.
Give your best anyway.
In the final analysis, it is between you and God.
It was never between you and them anyway.

CHAPTER 17

FINISHING WELL

THE JOURNEY IN THE SCHOOL OF LIFE TO FINISH WELL IS wide open. It takes an open heart to real surrender, open ears to real faith, open eyes to real vision and open understanding so that real freedom and wholeness on the inside is the outcome we finish with: *Loving others with clean love.*

I want to finish well, and I want you to finish well. I want to leave you with the inheritance of faith, hope, and love. Before this book comes to a close, I invite you to come with me to my secret sacred place. It's a place that I treasure and love to go alone, but I welcome you to come along. This sacred place is where I am real, raw, and vulnerable. In the midst of a rushing world, a place of peace is vital. Many days I can miss accessing that peace because of the *call to it all*. But when I go to my secret place, I know I'm safe. I go to my secret place at night because the busyness of the day captures me. This place holds the secrets to my *faith-field*. It's at night on a small cement step in the back of my house where I go to sit on my throne of grace. The darkness gives me the view of the night sky. I go there to leave the noise of the day that captured all of my attention and thoughts to listen to the sounds of the night. I look up and count the stars, and stare at the moon, and it brings me back to what childlike faith really feels like. Resident fireflies spark lights like fireworks and moths dance to the symphony of crickets. Brief staring matches happen with a passing raccoon. In every season it tells me the truth. The sound of rain tells me He opens the heavens and the Rainmaker pours out water to help me grow. The snow covers the earth to remind me of the cleansing of my sin. Even the moon says, *let there be light* to bring hope to any darkness; the leaves of the trees clap in the wind and bring me healing.

The air is never the same on any evening. It waits for me to throw my caution and fears of the day into the wind of the night. I center myself to adjust to the vulnerability of being honest to God; He knows anyway. Maybe because I feel small under the canopy of the night sky is why He feels so big. I know everything in me is exposed to Him. What was so important hours before has no hold on me now. This sacred place is the place where I can feel what I really truly feel. There is no tension, stress, hurry or hesitation—I can just be. It's the place I feel most accepted by God no matter what I may have previously been thinking, feeling, or doing.

The day can exhaust my hope, but at night my field of dreams becomes my reality. It's the place where everything is possible. It's in these minutes and moments, nothing can steal my treasure of feeling the significance of life. My attention is all right there in the moment and I am captured by the peace of the quiet orchestra of creation playing the song of deliverance over me. Love is the need of every human and in this special place the clean love of His presence is a present. There is nothing that I have to do to earn it, nothing that I say that can change it, nothing that I do that will offend it and nothing that can stop it. God's clean love invades my soul. I can rest in the assurance there is a bigger plan and I'm reassured again and again that everything is going to be all right.

To you, my new friend, thanks for coming. I hope you find your place of peace with God under His waterfall of clean love. You're worth it.

Waterfalls

> Lord, here I stand, humbled and amazed,
> underneath your waterfalls of love, Holy love.
> Change my heart, oh God,
> Fill me with Your glory.
> Change my heart, oh God,
> Fill me with Your Spirit,
> Wash me in Your love.
> I'm under Your showers, under Your blessings,
> I'm under the waterfalls of mercy and of grace.
> Change my heart oh God,
> Fill me with Your glory.
> Change my heart, oh God,
> Fill me with your Spirit,
> Wash me in your Love.
> Under the showers, under the blessings,
> Under the waterfalls of mercy and of grace.

CHAPTER 18

DECLARE IT

A FEW YEARS AGO, I CREATED THE DECLAREIT APP BECAUSE I wanted to encourage people. (www.declareitapp.com) It is an app used to combat negative thoughts using true declarations. Declareit app gives you the tools to align yourself with words that hold the keys to renewal and restoration of your mind, body, and spirit. Changing negative thoughts about yourself will change your world and mine.

The following is a written love letter for you to declare God's love, to flourish your life and fill your heart with clean love. Please read this section out loud; faith comes by hearing. Hear yourself Declare it.

I declare success over my life today. I declare I will experience the love and faithfulness of God. The favor of the Lord is upon me and my future is filled with hope and goodness.

I declare the blessings and promises of God in my life. Increase of hope, joy, and peace are mine as I experience His love. The plans God has for me are way above and beyond anything I've dreamed of, and I declare I trust Him to work it all out.

I declare strength, faith, and determination over me,

which means I have power. There is nothing too hard for God. I have perseverance, which promises hope and outlasts every challenge, blockage, and difficulty. I declare I am an overcomer. I will not worry and I will not doubt. I choose faith over fear, life over death, and hope over discouragement.

I declare that I will take nothing for granted—not people or opportunities. I declare that I will look at what I have and not at what I don't have—looking at what's right and not at what's wrong. My attitude has gratitude and faith. I am making right choices and living in integrity and excellence. I declare I am thriving.

I declare the wisdom of proverbs over my life. (Which means I have to read the book of Proverbs.) My circumstances may not always be easy and I may not always understand, but God is directing my every step. He's working out the details and his timing is perfect. I declare that everything will be all right.

I declare supernatural doors open for me today. He will connect me with the right people. I will be in the right place at the right time. I will let God fight my battles. I declare I will receive healing, opportunities, restoration, and breakthroughs.

I declare that I will see myself as God sees me—uniquely and wonderfully made. I declare that I believe that God believes in me and I am his masterpiece. I am beautiful, talented, and amazing, and I will do great things. I declare that I am right on time to accomplish all that is in my heart. I am creative and have good ideas. I declare success. This is my time and this is my moment.

I declare that I have a sound mind and I am not confused. I am more than equipped. I am anointed and empowered and God guides my thoughts.

I declare that I am the hands, feet, and mouthpiece for God. I encourage, I restore, and I have compassion and kindness. I am someone's miracle.

I declare I will pray with expectation, and I won't give up. Every promise and everything God created me to do I will become.

I declare right now that every curse and every negative word that has ever been spoken over me is broken in the mighty name of Jesus. I declare that there are no negative residual effects left. I declare I am happy, I am holy, I am healthy, and I am at peace.

I declare that I will use my words wisely—speaking life, favor, and victory. There are three words I must use most, and I must speak them with intention, understanding, and belief because I mean them. I will speak them to myself, to others, and to God. These words are: I Love You. I declare nothing can stop me.

Notes

Preface

All of our self-efforts and self-solutions . . . Ginger Harrington, p.xx.

Love's soul secret to prospering is resting in God . . . Ginger Harrington, p.xx.

Introduction

"Love is the key . . ." David Wagner, p.3.

My words will never pass away . . . Matt. 24:35 *World English Bible,* WEB, p.3.

Chapter 1

As children copy their fathers . . . J.B. Phillips, New Testament in Modern English (New York: Touchstone, 1996), p.8.

Love is patient, love is kind . . . 1 Cor. 13:4–8, NIV®, p.10.

Chapter 2

"BEHAVIOR NEVER EVER LIES" Richard Flint, Behavior Never Lies (Newport News, VA: Flint Inc., 2008), p.16.

A man who isolates himself . . . Prov. 18:1 *Spirit Filled Life Bible: New King James Version*, p.16.

Chapter 3

Consider it pure joy . . . James 1:2–4 NIV®, p.30.

Chapter 4

Out of a man's mouth . . . Matt.15:18, p.33

Where is wisdom? . . . Adapted from Job 28: 12–14 23–28. Interpretation by Gina Blaze, p.34.

Their minds are dull and slow to perceive . . . Matt. 13:15 The Passion Bible, p.36.

But it is the spirit in a person . . . Job 32:8 *Spirit Filled Life Bible: New King James Version, p.37.*

Chapter 6

Of those, 80 percent are negative and 95 percent are repetitive . . . This statistic originally comes from the National Science Foundation. For more on this, see "80% of Thoughts Are Negative…95 % are repetitive." March 12, 2012 by Faith Hope and Psychology. www. faithhopeandpsychology.wordpress.com, p.49.

As a man thinks, so he is . . . Prov. 23:7, p.49.

Today is the day the Lord has made . . . Ps. 118:24, p.49.

He makes me lie down . . . Ps. 23:2, p.50.

Chapter 7

For this people's heart has grown callous . . . Matt. 13:15
World English Bible, WEB, p.55.

Chapter 8

Create in me a clean heart . . . Ps. 51:10 *World English
Bible,* WEB, p.61.

Kindness makes a man attractive. . . Prov. 19:22. *Living
Bible,* TLB, p.64

Let him deny himself. . . Matt. 16:24 *World English
Bible,* WEB. p.65.

To repeat a matter . . . Prov. 17:9, p.66.

Where there are many words . . . Prov. 10:19, p.67.

It's like drinking poison . . . Paraphrased from St.
Augustine, p.69.

All you need for a dysfunctional family . . . Mary Karr,
The Liars Club: A Memoir (New York: Penguin, 2005),
p.69.

"If you cannot get rid of the family skeleton . . ." George
Bernard Shaw, p.69.

"When it becomes more difficult . . ." Quote by Robert
Anthony, p.73.

Swimming story credits to Rabbi Peter Oliveira, p.77.

Chapter 9

Gary Smalley once taught on personalities . . . For more on this, see the Smalley Institute www.smalleyinstitute.com, p.83.

Whether you already know Him . . . —Dan Lee, p.86.

You will seek me and find me . . . Jeremiah 29:13, p.86.

Chapter 10

Those who are wise will shine like the brightness . . . Daniel 12:3, p.91.

Chapter 11

Jesus prayed for unity: "Not for these only do I pray, but for those . . . John 17:20–21 *World English Bible,* WEB, p.102.

The gift of tears . . . For more on "the gift of tears" see Alan W. Jones *Soul Making: The Dessert Way of Spirituality* (New York: HarperCollins 1985). Dr. Jones is an Episcopalian priest and was Dean Emeritus of Grace Cathedral in San Francisco, p.103.

You are uniquely and wonderfully made . . . Ps. 139:14, p.109.

The Favor of the Lord is upon you . . . Ps. 90:17 and Ps. 84:11, p.109.

Chapter 12

The shame of life would be leaving this earth without doing what you were born to do . . . (Source not found), p.115.

Your career is what you're paid for . . . Quote by Steve Harvey, p.115.

Chapter 14

Prayer is communication with God for the intervention in humanities affairs. . . —Cindy Trimm, p.125.

The place of prayer is the most confident place we can go. . . .(Source not found), p.126.

"If the church is going to be visited by the angel of glory . . ." Jeremiah Johnson, *Judgment on the House of God: Cleansing and Glory Are Coming* (Shippensburg, PA: Destiny Image Publishers Inc., 2020), p.127.

Chapter 15

Horizontal and vertical honor —anthropologist Frank Henderson Stewart, p.131.

Chapter 17

Waterfalls, author unknown, p.143.

About the Author

Erica Carryl/Vine & Branch Photography

Gina Blaze is the cofounder and codirector of the New England Prayer Center (NEPC), a nonprofit ministry in Easton, Connecticut.

Gina is also a motivating and engaging life coach and a dynamic public speaker who is passionate about delivering messages of hope and healing. She is a people builder, highly encouraging, passionate to enact genuine change in peoples lives through identification of false belief about themselves.

"Coaching has changed me. I am willing to be transparent as it affects the outcome of others' lives. My conviction is that courage, determination and willingness will win the day. I have learned that no matter what people believe about themselves, it's ok—because God believes in them, and that real truth changes everything. It's been a gift to coach hundreds of people individually and thousands corporately. I have learned that we can miss the day by allowing our minds to live in yesterday or tomorrow. Today is the only day we have. It's the twenty-four hour gift that is right here and right now. What I bring to the table is my belief and my passion to celebrate, enjoy, and work hard this day and to love unconditionally. You can come just the way you are."

Gina is also the accomplished author of *Provoking Thoughts*, a collection of fifty-two encouraging weekly devotions designed to recharge and renew your thinking and creator of the "Declareit app"—a downloadable digital application that provides word notifications on Android and iPhone platforms to renew and restore your body, mind, and spirit.

Provoking Thoughts
by Gina Blaze

52 weekly reflections designed to
provoke thoughts about life.
There is one for every week.
Encouragement to recharge,
refine and rethink!

Available on amazon.com

THE DECLAREIT APP

The Declareit App has the ability to affect and combat negative thoughts using true declarations and affirmations! This amazing App gives you the tools to align yourself with words that hold the keys to renewal and restoration of your mind, body, and spirit.

Its like having a private coach in the palm of your hand!

- Delareit App brings instant encouragement, causing negative thought to be replaced and positive thought to be realized.
- Declareit App gives you wisdom, using declarations from categories of body and health, mind and emotions, faith, motivational, and intentional declarations with stunning backdrops.
- You can program the Declareit App to remind you once a day, once an hour, or every 15 minutes—you choose! Or . . . create your own declarations, then Declareit!

Over 350 million people worldwide suffer from depression/anxiety disorders, making it the most common mental disorder in the United States. The components of the mind, body, and spirit are interconnected. An imbalance in any of these areas can contribute and trigger these disorders. If you are struggling in any area—mind, body, or spirit, combat your struggle with Declareit App and keep profound words of truth front and center.

declareitapp.com

Changing negative thoughts will change your world and mine!